821

DEVELOPING RESPONSE TO POETRY

Open University Press

English, Language, and Education series

General Editor: Anthony Adams

Lecturer in Education, University of Cambridge

This series is concerned with all aspects of language in education from the primary school to the tertiary sector. Its authors are experienced educators who examine both principles and practice of English subject teaching and language across the curriculum in the context of current educational and societal developments.

TITLES IN THE SERIES

DEVELOPING RESPONSE TO POETRY

Patrick Dias and Michael Hayhoe

Open University Press
Milton Keynes · Philadelphia

Open University Press
Open University Educational Enterprises Limited
12 Cofferidge Close
Stony Stratford
Milton Keynes MK11 1BY

and
242 Cherry Street
Philadelphia, PA 19106, USA

First published 1988

British Library Cataloguing in Publication Data

Dias, P.
  Developing a response to poetry. –
  (English, language and education series).
  1. English literature – Study and
  teaching (Secondary)
  I. Title   II. Hayhoe, Mike   III. Series
821'.007'12   PR33

ISBN 0-335-15833-1

Library of Congress Cataloging-in-Publication Data

Dias, Patrick.
  Developing response to poetry.

  (English, language, and education series)
  Includes index.
  1. English poetry – Study and teaching (Secondary)
I. Hayhoe, Mike.   II. Title.   III. Series.
PR504.5.D5   1988   821'.007'12   87-34755
ISBN 0-335-15833-1 (pbk.)

Typeset by Vision Typesetting
Printed in Great Britain by the Alden Press, Oxford

Contents

General editor's introduction

One of the most common experiences my initial teacher training students have on their PGCE course is that of going to a school for teaching practice and being asked to teach some poetry – as 'we haven't done any lately'. My own observations suggest that there is a considerable unease in the case of many teachers of English, especially at secondary level, about what exactly to do with poetry in the classroom and that, in consequence, relatively little poetry is used, particularly in the first three years of secondary schooling. Yet it is difficult to think of any element within the English programme more suited to that age-range in the issues it raises and the linguistic extension of which it can be capable. It is also difficult to think of a time when there were more excellent poetry anthologies on the market, many of them within a price range that is still accessible to schools.

It was for these reasons that I very much wanted to include a book on the teaching of poetry in this series. We had already published Burgess and Gaudrey's *Time for Drama* and this seemed to meet a need, even though there were already a good number of books on drama teaching on the market. With a few exceptions, however, consideration of poetry teaching in book form is still much neglected, most of the best practical advice has tended to appear in articles which are, by their very nature, difficult to lay one's hands on.

The other stimulus to the present publication was the useful, though sparse, DES publication: *Teaching Poetry in the Secondary School: An HMI View* which is quoted in the first chapter. This is humane and contains much useful insight into practice but confirms the view, based on HMI visits, that poetry is on the defensive in many of our schools. The Inspectors found that 'in national terms, poetry is frequently neglected and poorly provided for . . . The message that children receive about poetry is clear enough: it comes a poor third behind the "For written answers" section and "Find out more about" demands.' It is often relegated to 'the end of the day or the week or the term, when resistance is low and all the "essential business" of English had been completed.'

As we move into a period in England and Wales of an ever more utilitarian and instrumental view of education this tendency is likely to be reinforced. In spite of the fact that the Secretary of State for Education and Science is himself an anthologist, we may suspect that the place of poetry within a nationally agreed 'core curriculum' will be a severely limited one. We may wonder, too, how the new curriculum overseers in the form of governors and parents will regard the place of poetry in the English programme. There is a real danger that, along with much of drama, music and art, this element in the English curriculum will be something that can be seen as expendable, when other, more obviously fruitful things, have to fight for their place in the curriculum and their space in the timetable.

My own observations abroad tend to support those of HMI in this country. In many visits to classrooms in four continents I have seen little evidence of poetry as a vital element within classroom practice; in many national and international conferences there has been little place for the discussion of the teaching of poetry on the learned agendas to do with reading and writing, talking and listening.

This is one reason why I sought out an international collaboration on the present volume. The two authors have been known to me for many years as amongst those who have resisted the limited value often placed on poetry in schools. As well as holding clear, and not dissimilar, theoretical perspectives on the nature and use of poetry in the school, they have also, by their own teaching, done much to generate good classroom practice in this area. Poetry is universal, possibly mankind's oldest expression of himself in language, and the authors have sought to make this book mirror this universal consideration. Thus, although I have begun this introduction by reference to the local (in terms of time and place) British scene, an important chapter in the book looks at the state of poetry teaching in the English speaking world as a whole and provides a listing of resources that can be used to widen the range of poetry that we use in our classrooms. Increasingly, as our own society in the UK becomes more culturally complex, and as the world shrinks its barriers through increased and improved communication, it becomes important for us to cease to think merely of English literature but to extend this to 'literature in English'. Few elements of this literature are more easily accessible than poetry and readers will note a commonality of concern amongst the various contributors to the international perspective of this volume.

In a sense the main progenitor of the present volume is Patrick Dias with whom many of those who attend conferences on English teaching in different parts of the world will be familiar. I first observed his work in Quebec in 1979 and I was struck then by the techniques which Patrick was using to help pupils become more articulate about their own responses to the poetry that they read. It seemed to me that, apart from the important theoretical work that was being developed about how young people make sense of poetry, there were also valuable implications for classroom practice at all levels of schooling. Since then I have had the privilege of seeing a good deal more of this work and, to a limited extent, been able to participate in it myself. I think that the insistence that the starting point must be the students' own spoken responses is a valuable one and one which gives an immediate lead into good classroom work. (It is amazing how much reliance had been placed by earlier researchers into written, rather than spoken, responses). Some of this work is helpfully explored in the present volume; those readers who need more detail are referred to Patrick Dias' recent research monograph (1987) published by the Canadian Council of Teachers of English: *Making Sense of Poetry – Patterns in the Process* – and it is with the nature of 'process reading' and 'process response' that the research is concerned and, out of which, the concerns of the present book grow.

With a British publisher in mind for the book I was anxious to find a collaborator who would share the same concerns and who had the necessary knowledge of what was happening in British schools. For this, my colleague, Mike Hayhoe of the University of East Anglia, was an obvious choice, and I was delighted when he was able to accept our invitation to write the book together with Patrick Dias. The book has grown over the last two years in terms of their growing knowledge of each other as scholars and teachers; over several meetings between them as authors, frequently with myself as General Editor, and I have watched its growth with fascination. I do not think either of the authors would deny that the book as it has emerged is not one that either could have written alone. It is itself a manifestation of the value of collaborative talk around a shared theme that so much underlies the whole approach indicated in the book. The subject has been limited to poetry and we much need (for reasons explored earlier) a book on this topic but, ultimately, it is about more than this – it is about a style of thinking about and practising the teaching of English that puts people in the centre and that sees the experience and enjoyment of poetry as itself a central part of this. It is a book much needed in a bleak age.

Anthony Adams

Introduction

This book is concerned primarily with presenting arguments for a re-examination of the ways in which poetry is taught in the secondary classroom. Over the last decade, our understanding of the nature of the transaction that occurs between a reader and a literary work has been helped considerably by recent theoretical work and research in the areas of response to literature and reading as well as by recent developments in literary critical theory. These more recent understandings have made those of us who work with adolescent readers far more aware of the complexity of those transactions and increasingly sensitive to the disjunction between how we understand the act of reading literature and how poetry is sometimes taught. In other words, the theory of reading literature that can be inferred from classroom practice is often at odds with what is understood about how most people actually read poetry. Such a re-examination is also in line with a general concern among teachers of English about how the ways in which pupils learn and teachers teach may be more helpfully aligned.

Such an awareness not only makes us wary of advancing immediate and simple solutions to the question of how teachers engage adolescents as readers of poetry; it also alerts us to the constraints on genuine engagement that classroom contexts often impose. This book is an attempt to take account of these more recent understandings of response to literature with a fuller awareness of the classroom contexts within which such responses are usually sought.

We begin by considering some of the issues that have brought about a book such as this. These pertain largely to the sets of beliefs, the prevailing literary critical notions that direct the teaching of poetry in secondary classrooms. These beliefs are, of course, not separate from a complementary set of convictions about the place of poetry, the roles of teachers and pupils, and how pupils' response to poetry must be evaluated. We go on to consider current critical theories in so far as they touch on the relationships between readers and literary texts and how the teaching of poetry might be informed by such theory. What can teachers take from developments in literary critical theory over the past 50 years? How relevant to classroom practice are the current assertions of Post–structuralist and Deconstructive criticism? What can we learn from Reader Response critics? How do we distinguish among the varying positions they represent on the role of readers in the literary transaction?

In Chapter 2 we consider how our understanding of the act of reading poetry can be informed by Reading and Discourse Processing theory and research. These fields offer several notions that help to explain what occurs in the transaction between readers and poems, and confirm the active role of readers and the transactional nature of reading. Chapter 3 reports on research on reader-response that is particularly applicable to the teaching of poetry. Again, research findings bear out the centrality of the reader's role in the making of meaning. They confirm as well how important it is that the contexts for reading poetry assign responsibility to readers for the meanings they make. Chapter 4 provides the transcripts of four readings by adolescents of Ted Hughes' 'The Thought-Fox'. These transcripts not only document how individual readers differ in the ways they go about making sense of a poem but also demonstrate the real abilities of adolescents as readers of poetry.

What then are the implications of such theory and research for classroom practice? Chapter 5 attempts to provide an answer to that question, taking account of our understandings of the nature of poetry, the act of reading, and the real capabilities of adolescent readers. For instance, what does it mean in practice for teachers to assert the autonomy of pupils as readers of poetry? How can teachers and classrooms cultivate responsive and responsible reading? Chapter 6 expands this discussion to consider developments in four countries. The contributors to this discussion are familiar with the state of poetry teaching in their respective countries and provide heartening information that some of the central issues described in this book are at the core of discussion – and action – in their own countries. What is particularly useful in this chapter are the lists of resources – print, audio-visual and human – that are appended to each of their reports.

Acknowledgements

We are grateful to Ken Watson, Brian Hirst, Coralie Bryant, and Susan Tchudi for their contributions to Chapter 6. Their gracious and prompt responses to our requests are most appreciated. We are particularly grateful to pupils who participated in the study described in Chapter 4, and thank them, their teacher John Blanchard, and the administration of Comberton Village College, Cambridgeshire for always affording a warm welcome and easy access to the facilities and resources of the College. Some of the research described in this study was supported by grants from the Social

Sciences and Humanities Research Council of Canada, McGill University's Social Sciences Research Grants Committee and the School of Education of the University of East Anglia. We thank these agencies and also the British Council whose financial support helped make possible the travel that allowed us to collaborate on this book. We thank as well Anthony Adams who encouraged us in this joint endeavour and the ELSID English Teaching Group whose discussions on putting theory into practice contributed so much to Chapter 5. Above all we wish to thank our respective spouses, Patricia Dias and Jean Hayhoe, who have put up patiently with the single-mindedness that overcomes some academics who try to write a book in their spare time.

Parts of Chapter Four have appeared in *The English Quarterly* (published by the Canadian Council of Teachers of English) and in *English in Education* (published by the National Association of Teachers of English in the UK) and are gratefully acknowledged.

An extract from 'The Thought-Fox' from *The Hawk in the Rain* by Ted Hughes is reprinted by permission of Faber and Faber Limited, London and Harper & Row, New York.

An extract from *The Snake Trying* by W. W. E. Ross is reprinted by permission of Academic Press, Canada.

1 Theories of criticism: their influence on classroom practice

In considering the state of poetry teaching in secondary schools we can point to several signs which indicate that poetry is alive and well. The last decade or so has seen the publication of several anthologies of poetry for secondary school pupils, anthologies that are appealing to adolescent readers both in format and content. There are a number of recent books that describe exciting ways of involving pupils in the writing of poetry. In our own visits to schools we have come across several instances of innovative ways of teaching poetry and felt a general concern among teachers of English that poetry matters and ought to hold a central place in the English curriculum.

On the other hand there are reasons not to be complacent about the state of poetry teaching. We have such disconcerting assertions as Greeves' in the *Times Educational Supplement*, 19 September 1986, p. 22: 'Poetry has become so rare in schools that it ought to be put on the endangered list.' And a recent report from Her Majesty's Inspectorate in Great Britain confirms that such a view is not just individual opinion:

> Inspection of and visits to secondary schools indicate that there is in many of them very little poetry included regularly in the work in English. The findings of specialist one day visits and a number of full inspection reports show that poetry was at the centre of work in English for rather less than five per cent of the English lessons observed. The evidence is that, in national terms, poetry is frequently neglected and poorly provided for; its treatment is inadequate and superficial. . . .
>
> Some English teachers express great unease about teaching poetry and it appears that there are few genuine enthusiasts who read poetry extensively themselves and communicate that enthusiasm to pupils. (Department of Education and Science, 1987, pp. 4–5)

It will become clear in the final chapter that such a description applies to countries other than Britain as well. It seems that whatever advances have occurred in the state of poetry teaching, they have not been sufficient or widespread enough to make a noticeable impact on classroom practice in general, and that we are still faced with attitudes to poetry among adolescents that are fairly represented by one 15-year-old Cambridgeshire comprehensive school pupil: 'Well, in school if someone said we are going to read a poem, you think, "Ah, this is gonna be dead boring".'

There is no one cause for poetry being unpopular in some secondary schools. One can cite past practice such as forced memorization and recitation, and a selection of poems for classroom study decided largely by anthologists' didactic and conservative concerns. But such practices are largely in the past and anthologies of poetry published over the last 15 years are appealing both in the range and the 'contemporariness' of the poems they offer. Our contention is that a prime cause of the unpopularity of poetry in the classroom lies in the critical theory that is implicit in much teaching of poetry in secondary schools. There are three major trends in literary criticism that have affected and continue to affect poetry teaching: (1) New Criticism, (2) Structuralism and (3) Post-structuralism. It is important that we understand how these theories impinge on our teaching of poetry and how the practices they give rise to are likely to alienate adolescent readers or win them over to the reading of poetry.

New Criticism and classroom practice

Until recently, the teaching of poetry, both at university and in schools has been dominated by the conception of a poem as an object that can and must be closely analysed. Such a view, whether it is called objective or formalist, sees the apprehension of a poem as a process of close reading, a careful attending to the words on the page, an 'explication', to borrow the French term. Such an approach, as it has filtered down to the secondary school classroom through teachers themselves trained in the close reading of literary text, has led to classes in poetry where the sole object is one of training pupils to read poetry by examining as many aspects as would explain its inner workings. That approach still persists, even if only to meet the requirements of school leaving examinations, as witness the ample documentation provided by Dixon and Brown (1985).

Such an 'objective' or 'formalist' approach (which one might add is characteristic of the New Criticism school which dominated literary study, particularly in North America, through the late 1930s and into the 1960s) takes little account of the reader's role in the making of meaning or, for that matter, of the author's intentions and context. The 'poem' is self-contained and autonomous. To regard the work in terms of its effects on the reader is to be guilty of the 'affective fallacy'; guilty of confusing the poem with its effects. To consider the design or intention of the author, however derived, in judging the success or determining the meaning of a literary work is to have fallen victim to the 'intentional fallacy' (see Wimsatt, 1958).

This is not to say that this view of literature as an 'object' has been rigidly enforced in the secondary classroom. However, in discussing a poem there is a tendency for teachers to advert to the authority of the text and to discount the experiences evoked in readers by the poem or the information relevant to the context within which the poem was written or set. It is primarily the devaluing of the role of the reader, of what one might call the 'subjective response', that concerns us here; for it has had major consequences for how teachers have perceived their roles as purveyors of poetry and for how neophyte readers of poetry have been regarded.

If it is believed that meaning resides largely or even entirely in the text, it follows that pupils can be taught how to get at meaning by careful or close reading. To quote from *Freedom and Discipline in English* (1965, p. 56), an influential report of the Commission on English (a distinguished panel of scholars and educators convened by the College Entrance Examination Board in the United States): 'When he has the text before him, a good reader makes a deliberate effort to keep intrusive thoughts and feelings out of the way of what the text is saying.' By stressing 'what the text is saying' and discounting the reader's thoughts and feelings (however intrusive), the statement is fairly representative of the then prevailing critical view. In the report, the critic's role is to model such 'disinterested' reading, and the teacher's role becomes one of serving pupils as a mediator, one whose role is to train pupils into a style of 'objective' reading.

It is not surprising that such a role is so easily assumed. It is consistent with the role of teacher as informed dispenser of information about literature, and is also consistent with the role teachers are expected to assume in most other subject areas. It supports an examining system that demands from pupils the one correct reading and rewards them for it. Thus it is that the authors of *Freedom and Discipline* can suggest:

> One part of what the good English teacher knows, then, by wide and discriminating reading and study, is literature. But, in a perfectly practical sense, he cannot fully impart it. Only the student, by many acts of understanding and liking, can make the literature he reads his own. What can the teacher do about literature? He can talk about works expertly, ask questions about them, discuss them, think highly of them, and show his students how to think, talk, and write about what they read (pp. 54–5).

The role assigned the teacher as model and expert mediator between text and reader is, we would argue, more a deterrent to readers' achieving an autonomy as readers than it is a help. It can hardly allow even the most confident student to make 'the literature he reads his own', as the report of the Commission on English piously hopes. The pupil is placed in the role of apprentice reader, inadequate and subject to all the ten pitfalls that Richards sketched out in *Practical Criticism* (1929). We might note in passing that Richards in assessing his readers' protocols was doing so as an expert reader. In describing their readings as inadequate, excessive, or inappropriate, he was positing norms from which they had deviated. That the teacher as expert reader somehow acquires these norms and applies them dispassionately in the classroom is at heart the stance that defeats the development of adolescent readers who might speak confidently and responsibly from their own responses to the text.

Such a stance dictates that a teacher's role is to *conduct* the reading of the poem, and hope somehow that his or her reading will be appropriated by pupils. It dictates a classroom procedure which operates primarily through a process of inductive questioning by the teacher and a corresponding developing sense of the poem by the pupils. The teacher is in charge of the meaning that evolves, and the text, rather than the readers' generally unverifiable (it seems) impressions and intuitions, must be adduced in support of the meaning that is 'unlocked' through the teachers' questioning. To borrow an analogy that Graves (1981) has used in speaking of how writing is often taught, the teacher, the keeper of the poem, 'owns' the poem, the children merely 'rent' it. They live (so to speak) in the poem on the owner's terms; for the poem is not theirs to 'mess around in'.

It is indeed ironic that the teacher's questions are often not real questions; that is, they are not questions to which the answers are not already known, questions that arise from genuine curiosity and promote inquiring. And these questions are generally not the pupils' questions. Rather, they are questions that programme a particular direction of inquiry and a particular destination. Readers, in effect, will have arrived without really having travelled, as Barnes (1976) puts it; that is, without having observed and inspected the sites along the way and without having been led astray by ambiguous signs, intriguing side-trips and frustrating dead-ends. Being led astray and being frustrated is not really problematical if we consider reading, as Craig (1976, p. 35) puts it, 'as a possible adventure which in prospect disquiets some, attracts others'.

There is a price pupils always pay for the convenience of 'packaged' tours: because they are not expected to make sense of a poem for themselves, they are unlikely to learn to 'travel' on their own. If we continue along the lines of this analogy, tour operators and guides soon lose sight of why people wish to travel. The packaging becomes a virtue and a tour's sole selling point.

For many teachers, the act of transferring responsibility to their pupils for the meanings they make causes great moral unease and is seen as a thin disguise for abdicating responsibility for what their pupils learn. And where teachers have begun to transfer to pupils responsibility for their readings, we sense that some of them are not prepared to let go fully, wishing to retain some degree of control over their pupils' readings. They are probably taking too much account of the comments of uninformed critics who see such authorizing of readers as symptomatic of an anything-goes, *laissez faire* attitude among teachers.

One of the more urgent reasons for this book is to present a coherent basis for response-centred teaching, a basis argued from current literary-critical theory and research on reader response and from our own observations and studies of pupils' responses to poetry. We are aware of the difficulties involved in implementing a response-centred programme and will argue that a concern to authorize readers as autonomous readers of poetry defines the teacher's role in ways that are even more challenging and responsible than have been implicit in teacher-centred lessons. In what follows we review briefly structuralist approaches to the study of literature in terms of their implications for the teaching of poetry.

Structuralist approaches to the study of poetry

New Criticism directed a pedagogy that promoted the close reading of poems as self-sufficient wholes, a pedagogy designed to help beginners in poetry reading become 'expert' readers and interpreters. The stress was on deriving interpretations by studying the internal structures of a poem, interpretations that could be supported by the text without adverting to readers' responses or to whatever extraneous information might assist in interpretation. While New Critical notions remain strongly embedded in much classroom practice, since the 1950s there have been major shifts in critical theory and practice that have most likely had some influence on our aims and methods in teaching poetry.

These shifts come under the general heading of structuralist approaches. There have been two general shifts. The first shift has been away from a focus on interpretation; the second has been away from the consideration of a 'poem' as an individual entity. The movement has been towards two things; first, an attempt to understand literature as an institution in our time and secondly, a concern to understand the general principles or structures by which literary works have 'meaning'. This new perspective sees individual acts of interpretation as instances of a system at work and the literary theorist's task as one of defining that system not only as it operates in individual works but also as it functions in the interrelationships among works. Structuralist theories of literature begin then with an assumption that literature, like language – a human artefact – is systematic; that is, it depends on regularities of forms and functions which are perceived as a system. Any disciplined study of literature therefore must base itself in a study of that system, just as linguistics, the study of language as a discipline, must draw primarily not on studies of individual instances of language use but on attempts to define the underlying structures, the 'deep structures', of language itself and the laws by which language works.

One set of such 'deep structures' is proposed by Frye in *Anatomy of Criticism* (1966), an attempt to provide a conceptual framework, a system of classification by modes, symbols, archetypes and genres that would apply to all literature. While Frye's work is far too comprehensive and various to fit under one or another label, we cite him as one of many critics whose endeavours clearly represent a search for a systematic poetics, rationales for a discipline of literature. Structuralist critics have begun to displace a criticism concerned with individual authoritative acts of interpretation by trying to create systems – the 'deep structures' – that help us view the vast range of writing offered as 'literature', some of which we may feel ambivalent about, within one or more accommodating frameworks. As Eagleton puts it, deep structures can be 'dug out of Mickey Spillane as well as Sir Philip Sidney, and no doubt the same ones at that' (1983, p. 107). A structuralist poetics seeks to find out how literary works have the meaning they do; and in doing so, may take fuller account of the cultural contexts within which literary works are produced and consumed.

Jonathan Culler (1983, p. 20) sums up how Structuralism diverges from the 'interpretive projects of the New Criticism':

> The interpretive projects of the New Criticism were linked to the preservation of aesthetic autonomy [we interpret this to mean that literary text is self-sufficient and has a consistency of meaning and affect that the reader must somehow arrive at] and the defense of literary studies against encroachment by various sciences. If, in attempting to describe the literary work, 'structuralist' criticism deploys various theoretical discourses, encouraging a kind of scientific encroachment, then critical attention comes to focus not on a thematic content that the work aesthetically presents but on the conditions of signification, the different sorts of structures and processes involved in the production of meaning. Even when structuralists engage in interpretation, their attempt to analyze the structure of the work and the forces on which it depends leads to concentration on the relation between the work and its enabling conditions and undermines, as the opponents of structuralism seem to sense, the traditional interpretive project.

The Structuralist agenda is ambitious. It asks readers to surrender their right to a personal response. It asks that they be more scientific and bring to their reading a knowledge of structures and forms. Readers may even need to resuscitate knowledge of the contexts within which the work was produced. Structuralism may provide a conceptual basis for the study of literature as a university discipline; however, the explicit and detailed analysis which Structuralism demands is clearly inappropriate in the secondary school. What Structuralism does invite at the secondary level is (1) a questioning of the traditional literature curriculum and its 'interpretive projects', (2) a consideration of how and why we value what we do teach as literature, and (3) a widening of the contexts within which literature, however defined, is studied. Such Structuralist approaches are apparent for instance in activities that involve pupils in examining literary texts for gender bias or narrative strategies. A Structuralist approach might substitute the classroom study of individual works with the task of elucidating and applying systems of literary meaning. For instance, using Propp's

(1970) analysis of narrative schemes in fairy tales (Propp proposed seven 'spheres of action' and 31 functions of character), pupils might attempt an analysis and classification of local folk tales. We are not necessarily advocating such exercises as much as providing an instance of how literature might be studied from a structural perspective.

This discussion of structuralist approaches to the study of literature may seem to be a diversion from our main effort to determine how particular literary critical positions direct the teaching of poetry in ways that often undermine teachers' efforts at developing competent autonomous readers. A Structuralist approach posits explicit analytical inquiry with the intention of arriving at some understanding of the systems by which literary works 'mean'. What is likely to alienate most adolescent readers is that such purist study views a literary work as part of an interrelated system of other works and thus tends to disvalue the responses that such a work has evoked. If inexperienced readers of literature are obliged to use an advanced structuralist approach, they are likely to believe that they cannot approach a literary work without having acquired some familiarity with the basic 'codes' and 'structures' that Structuralism identifies as helping such works function. They are also likely to believe that they cannot operate at all without some knowledge of the wider literary field from which these codes and structures derive. In these circumstances the pupils are still likely to ascribe to the teacher the role of identifying these structures and providing the wider literary frameworks, forcing the teacher to remain in the role of instructor, in charge of how a poem will be taught and how it will be received.

As was the case with New Critical approaches to poetry and as has been the case more recently with structuralist approaches, how poetry is taught in universities continues to provide tacitly a model for the aims and approaches that prevail in the secondary classroom. We believe it is such transferrings that have helped make the teaching of poetry marginal and disaffecting in many secondary classrooms. It is only as critical theory begins increasingly to take note of the role of readers in the making of meaning that we might see a significant shift in aligning critical theory with what we know of the ways adolescent pupils really read and learn.

Post-structuralist approaches to the study of poetry

In developing our argument for a radical shift in the ways poetry is taught in the secondary school, we have pressed for the need to examine the theoretical assumptions implicit in approaches to the teaching of poetry in most English classrooms. It has been suggested that both New Critical and Structuralist theories may be implicit in much classroom practice (and quite likely at odds) and can be reinforced both by institutional and societal expectations that pupils should receive knowledge of and about poetry and that teachers should transmit such knowledge, or at best mediate so that it can be called to account for examination purposes. In fact, both theoretical approaches are quite consistent with the kinds of demands for account-ability made in most examination questions. In effect, the demands of these theoretical approaches can impose on the teacher a degree of interventionist control over how poems are read and how meaning is made. The following sets out our reasons for believing that Post-structuralist critical theory may affect classroom practice in ways that are more consonant with ways young people actually read literature. By examining its assumptions and its likely implications for the teaching of poetry, we hope to ensure that whatever is derived from post-structuralist theory is at least not inconsistent with the practices we advocate towards developing autonomous readers of poetry.

Post-structuralism covers a range of critical activities far too diverse to be defined briefly. Our account can only be reductive and incomplete; but it aims at describing those aspects of Post-structuralist thinking that are likely to have some relevance for classroom practice and will allow teachers to recognize and place particular developments in the literature curriculum and, if necessary, redefine their roles as teachers of poetry.

To an extent, Post-structuralism may be defined by its opposition to Structuralism, by a scepticism aimed at undermining the efforts at certainty implied by the Structuralist agenda. It questions the implication in Structuralist theory that competent readers, like competent users of language, must have a knowledge of the literary code that allows them access to literary meaning in a consistent way. Whether such literary competence is innate or acquired or both is not at issue. Post-structuralists would deny the degree of certainty implied by a notion that structures of meaning are stable and present objectively in literary texts. They argue two key points. First, meaning in language is not the stable thing that most traditional critics have implied. Secondly, an observer's mind is inevitably tied to the realities she or he observes, so that 'objectivity' is always in question. Given the provisionality of language and the subjectivity of all perception, Post-structuralist criticism sets out to look at literary text as a human enterprise which is not from the gods. It pays literary text the respect of questioning and arguing with it, including revealing its tensions, contradictions and implicit ideologies.

Post-structuralist or Deconstructive Criticism (the terms are often used synonymously) attends closely to the text as does the old 'New Criticism'. Unlike New Criticism, which sought to reconcile seeming opposites and disharmonies within the text into an organic whole, Post-structuralist criticism seeks to 'destabilize' the text as a secure object, including finding its gaps and demonstrating its indeterminacy. Our description may give the impression that we perceive Post-structuralism only as a programme of subversion and even destructiveness, but in fact it has positive aspects. By inviting and approving our consideration of alternative meanings and by looking at literary text as a dynamic entity, or to use its terminology, as being unstable, Post-structuralism argues for ways of reading that postpone closure, that allow for dwelling in uncertainty, and encourage an awareness of alternative meanings. There appears to be a recognition of a psychological reality that much of our interpretive thinking is unconscious and fragmentary and includes consideration of meanings that we are not consciously aware of. De Beaugrande cites J. Hillis Miller, an American Post-structuralist critic, as contending that a '"monological" mode of thought that makes each entity single-natured should yield to a "dialogical" one that allows an entity to be both itself and not itself but something else at the same time' (1984, p. 553).

Clearly much teaching of poetry over the years has tended to support the idea of convergence towards single meanings. By promoting the dialogical, Post-structuralist criticism has authorized the widely differing readings that can emerge in a classroom. Culler (1983), summarizing Derrida, suggests how literary text has a potential for multiple meaning:

> There is nothing that might not be put into a literary work; there is no pattern or mode of determination that might not be found there. To read a text . . . as literature is to remain attentive even to its apparently trivial features. A literary analysis is one that does not foreclose possibilities of structure and meaning in the name of the rules of some limited discursive practice (p. 182).

In the following chapters it should become clear that Derrida's stance towards literary text is a necessary part of a programme that recognizes the role of readers in the making of meaning and respects the varied contributions of readers in the dialogue of the classroom. Unfortunately, most published deconstructive readings are from the university world and far too 'clever' and 'academic' to convince people to use such an approach in the secondary classroom. Such readings can degenerate into interminable readings of readings, esoteric conversations solely for the informed and scholarly.

We assert that deconstructive reading need not be like this. It need not involve excessive poring over a text of the kind that some learned people practise. Post-structuralist criticism like any form of criticism asks a reader to attend. The following is an example of one of many ways of 'destabilizing', of recognizing the provisionality of a text. The poem, 'The Choice' is by the American writer, Dorothy Parker:

The Choice

He'd have given me rolling lands,
　　Houses of marble, and billowing farms,
Pearls, to trickle between my hands,
　　Smouldering rubies, to circle my arms.

You – you'd only a lilting song,
  Only a melody, happy and high,
You were sudden and swift and strong –
  Never a thought for another had I.

He'd have given me laces rare,
  Dresses that glimmered with frosty sheen,
Shiny ribbons to wrap my hair,
  Horses to draw me, as fine as a queen.
You – you'd only to whistle low,
  Gayly I followed wherever you led.
I took you, and I let him go –
  Somebody ought to examine my head!

Most readers would agree that the speaker having chosen her suitor for love rather than for money seems to be regretting her choice and the riches she has forfeited by that choice. We might spend some time deciding why we believe she does not really regret her choice. Having found our reasons, can we be so sure? Are we not assuming too easily that the poem is spoken only half-seriously, in a playful, self-mocking tone? What if we perceive the speaker as a disgruntled pensioner muttering half to herself and half to an obviously hung-over husband with a two-day growth to boot? We offer this example as a rather straightforward and only half-facetious instance of how to destabilize a text, not in order to discover the chimera of 'its true meaning' so much as to recognize a continuing doubt about the possibility of ever being sure. But as we shall come to argue later, we are *not* advocating deconstructive reading for its own sake. A tolerance of ambiguity and an awareness of the possibilities of meaning are key goals in helping unsure adolescent readers of poetry realize their full potential as readers.

Table 1 provides a summary chart of the polar stances of the critical developments presented thus far. We have offered only a partial and fragmentary account of some central developments in recent critical theory. In doing so, we have detailed just those aspects likely to have some consequences for the classroom teaching of poetry. It is hoped that this account will help teachers identify the theoretical issues that are implicit in the ways they go about teaching poetry. In other words, what theoretical positions are they working from? For us the core issues centre around the question of authority in interpretation. And since, in the theoretical developments we have described, the place of interpretation is increasingly in question, what kinds of classroom activities are legitimized by such critical developments?

We are aware of how the New Criticism's emphasis on 'meaning in the text' remains firmly embedded in classroom practice and in examination procedures. Structuralist influences will be felt not only in a stronger emphasis on literature as a system to be mastered, but also as arguments for a curriculum within which literature is no longer privileged, but is one mode

Table 1. Stances in critical theory

Theory	Place of 'meaning'	Critical activity
New Criticism	Meaning is in the text and is to be discovered; the text is guardian of the poem's meaning	Determine what the poem means and how it has transmitted its message
Structuralism	The Meaning of a particular poem is given less importance; the focus is on structures and systems of textual meaning	Determine the principle of the systems by which poems mean
Post-structuralism	Meaning is indeterminate and unstable – by the very arbitrariness of language and the individual 'subjectivities' of readers and writers	'Deconstructive' criticism – constructing and reconstructing; demonstrating how a poem cannot mean on its own or as part of a system, but is dependent on several choices on the part of its readers

of discourse among other discourse systems. Post-structuralist thinking can impinge most directly on classroom practice in a general recognition of the role of readers – even though the current models of Post-structuralist practice are generally expert readers possessed of a vast array of cultural and literary experience.

New Criticism authorizes the text; Structuralism, the systems and the conditions of meaning: 'the norms, conventions, and mental processes that account for meaning' (Culler, 1981, p. 11); Post-structuralism authorizes neither the reader nor the text, and denies the usefulness of a systematic theory or 'poetics' of meaning and interpretation. Instead, Post-structuralism legitimizes multiple interpretations and a continuing effort to question the status of the generally approved canon of school literature and its approved interpretations. It is clear that neither New Critical nor Structuralist theories attend to readers' roles in the creation of meaning; in fact, there appears to be a general distrust of 'lay' readers. New Criticism sets up critics as expert readers, conscientiously objective in their attendance to the text; those beginning to read poetry must profit from example. The Structuralist's role is again one of demonstration but with a far more extensive apparatus of norms and conventions. Post-structuralists as well can weigh readers down with their cleverness, their neat tricks of reversal, their picking and poking in the most unlikely places. Thus all three critical movements, to a greater or lesser extent, can enforce an attitude towards reading which disenfranchises the developing reader of poetry. Ironically, with the exception of some of the oldest school, the New Critics, there is at this stage little awareness that below university levels of study readers of poetry are very much non-specialist readers.

And it is precisely the role of the reader in the act of reading that has not been sufficiently and properly addressed in the critical movements we have described.

Towards reader-oriented criticism

It is really only since the late 1960s that literary criticism has shifted its attention away from a study of the poem as an entity in its own right or as an instance of the workings of a larger system of signification, to attend to the role of the reader. The literary work is much more than an object that exists in and of itself, much more than the creation of the literary artist; it is also the product of an act of reading and of readers.

There are several explanations for the shift from a more or less exclusive concern with textual meaning to a growing attention to the role of readers in literary reading. One of the more forceful influences may have been a general shift in the sciences and humanities from product-oriented towards process-oriented inquiry. In the study of literature such a move would be represented by a de-emphasising of the status of the literary work as an autonomous object and a redirection of attention to the act of reading: a shift from the product of reading to the process of reading. Such a shift also recognized the need to consider the physical, social, psychological, political and ideological contexts in which the phenomenon is to be studied. Moreover, possibly as a product of the social and political radicalism that emerged, for instance, on some university campuses in the late 1960s, much critical discussion focused on ideological issues that were implicit in literary production and the critical enterprise: literature as anodyne and critics as guardians of culture. For instance, while in 1959 the American poet and critic John Ciardi could ask *How Does a Poem Mean?* with an emphasis on the dominance of the text, in 1970, Walter Slatoff's *With Respect to Readers: Dimensions of Literary Response* could wittily signal the importance of the reader in contributing to meaning. A powerful influence in helping establish reader-response criticism as a legitimate and promising area of scholarly inquiry came with the importation into English Studies of a large body of Continental Structuralist and Post-structuralist criticism that had become part of the standard fare in most French Literature and Comparative Literature Departments in British and North American Universities. Such criticism provided a basis for studying literature as a cultural entity and a closer attendance to the processes involved in literary reading.

It is not that prior to the 1960s literary critics were unaware of the reader's active role. Even the influential British critic F. R. Leavis, who is certainly an advocate of close reading and of the autonomy of a literary work (he often cites Coleridge's dictum that a literary work must contain within itself the reason why it is so and not otherwise) feels it necessary to remind his readers: 'You cannot point to the poem; it is "there" only in the re-creative response of individual minds to the black marks on the page' (1962, p. 28) – an observation he first made in *Education and the University* (1948, p. 70). Such an acknowledgement of the reader's role is offered almost as an aside, a point in a larger argument; not as a move towards empowering readers. And the readers Leavis has in mind are members of an élite minority, 'the educated public'.

Even then, such reminders remain rare in literary critical writing prior to the 1960s; quite probably because they have not seemed pertinent to the critical approaches dominant at the time. For one thing, such recognitions of the reader are likely to subvert an insistence on the autonomy of the literary work. In their concern to demonstrate ideal readings, New Critics may have been less willing to authorize readers in any way other than as aspirants to a common set of understandings to be validated by the text. But there are exceptions.

One of the more prominent of such exceptions is Rosenblatt's affirmation, as early as 1938, in *Literature as Exploration*, of the active role of the reader in the making of meaning:

> The word *exploration* is designed to suggest primarily that the experience of literature, far from being for the reader a passive process of absorption, is a form of intense personal activity. The reader counts for at least as much as the book or poem itself; he responds to some of its aspects and not others; he finds it refreshing and stimulating, or barren and unrewarding.
>
> (Preface to the First Edition)

But we had to wait almost another three decades before discussions of readers' responses to literature became a noticeable issue in the critical literature. It is primarily as a pedagogical concern, as was the case with Rosenblatt in 1938, that the case for readers began to gain ground. In 1966, participants in the Anglo-American seminar on the Teaching of English (Dartmouth, New Hampshire) according to Dixon's (1967) report of that meeting, had identified three 'models or images of English':

> The first centred on *skills*: it fitted an era when initial literacy was the prime demand. The second stressed the *cultural heritage*, the need for a civilizing and socially unifying content. The third (and current) model focuses on *personal growth*: on the need to re-examine the learning processes and the meaning to the individual of what he is doing in English lessons (pp. 1–2).

There are interesting parallels between these models and the developments in literary critical theory we have been sketching. We have moved, certainly in literary studies, away from an almost exclusive concern with text (from philological investigations and New Critical close reading) and away from an overriding concern with establishing what belongs in the canon of English Literature and the Tradition, towards according greater consideration to the role of the reader in the literary transaction. From the Dartmouth Conference came a publication that fully exemplified the new focus: *Response to Literature* (Squire, 1968). In 1968 Rosenblatt's *Literature as Exploration* was reissued in a revised edition.

The new emphasis derives clearly from pedagogical concerns, generally an attempt to take fuller account of the reading processes of pupils and to make the curriculum more directly relevant to their needs and interests and less an instrument of institutional and societal demands. As was suggested above, such a move was consonant with the prevailing social climate. And the literary critical theory to support such developments was just beginning to emerge. Chapter 3 considers at some length the research on reader-response that has been generated by the need to inform classroom practice in the teaching of literature; while the following concludes this survey of recent and current critical theory that has direct bearing on the business of teaching poetry.

Reader-response criticism

Reader-response criticism, as it has come into prominence over the last two decades, represents far too broad a spectrum of critics and critical writing to define a single movement or school. A selective account, therefore, has been chosen which draws only on the work of those critics who typify the various developments in reader-response theory and whose positions clearly impinge on what occurs in classroom practice. These critics have been grouped together and their arguments will be discussed under three separate headings:

1 Readers in texts,
2 Texts in readers,
3 Between texts and readers.

Readers in texts

The focus of such criticism is on the reader within the text; that is, the reader implied or intended by the text. Criticism in this mode would seek to define the codes or conventions by which the reader is written into the text: Is the reader addressed directly or indirectly? How is the reader "created" or invoked by the text? Can actual readers function at two levels, submitting to becoming the reader implied by the work and being aware at the same time that they are subordinating their actual beliefs and values in the process? These and other such issues lead inevitably to an examination of the text; the focus again is on the structuralist question: 'How do texts have the meanings they do?'

This is essentially a reductive account of a position implicit in considerable and important work by literary theorists as various as Barthes (1974), Eco (1979), Ong (1975) and Riffaterre (1978). Yet, however challenging and interesting such questions might be, they remain currently the pursuit of academic readers. The main usefulness of such critical work for teachers lies in the possibilities it reveals of how texts can *act* on readers and invoke their collaboration: the text is seen as being 'proactive', making moves for the reader to follow. But that is only one side of the literary transaction; there are critics who dwell on the other partner in that transaction, the reader, as being more active.

Texts in readers

There are a few critics who argue that literary texts have their meaning primarily if not entirely in the subjective responses of readers. The foremost proponent of such a view is Holland, an American theorist who argues that reading 'can never be impersonal and objective' (1973, p. 117). Holland uses American ego psychology to demonstrate that an individual's reading is essentially a projection on the work of that individual's 'identity theme': a constant but dynamic construct that shapes response to the text (*5 Readers Reading*, 1975). In other words, meaning in reading is experienced uniquely by each reader and can be accounted for by that reader's psychic make-up:

> In reading, I bring to a text schemata from previous literary experiences, from my historical or critical knowledge, my sense of human nature, my values, my preferences in language, my politics, my metabolism – I bring all these things to bear on the text, and the text feeds back to me what I bring to it either positively or not at all. It rewards my hypotheses or, so to speak, ignores them. That is all the text does, for always it is I who am in control. It is I who ask questions of the text and I who hear and interpret its answers. The text may change the payoffs on the various fantasies, defenses, themes, or expectations I bring to it, but that is all it does (and even then I decide what is a good payoff and what is not).
>
> We cannot read without actively constructing the text before us, and that is why actual readings vary so much from one person to another. Reading is permeated with the uniqueness of your personality or mine . . . (1985, p. 7).

We may not agree entirely, but at least this subjectivist position points up the one-sidedness of the view that meaning is entirely embedded in and directed by the text and is independent of individual interpretation.

A moderate version of Holland's position is taken up by Bleich, who argues that a reader's interpretation of a literary text necessarily reflects that reader's subjective response to that text. 'To say that perceptual processes are different in each person is to say that reading is a wholly subjective process and that the nature of what is perceived is determined by the rules of the personality of the perceiver' (*Readings and Feelings*, 1975, p. 3). In his more comprehensive theoretical work, *Subjective Criticism* (1978), Bleich elaborates on this argument:

> An observer is a subject, and his means of perception define the essence of the object and even its existence to begin with. An object is circumscribed and delimited by a subject's motives, his curiosities, and above all, his language (p. 18).

In the case of literary reading, interpretation will reflect the reader's individuality, an interpretation to be validated by negotiation among a community of readers, that is, a process of resymbolization that produces knowledge. A legitimate criticism of Bleich's argument is that by his premises, even such resymbolization is eventually subjective and personal and its claim as 'knowledge' dependent on how that community of readers negotiates meaning. However, what is important for our purposes is Bleich's insistence that emotional reactions are an essential and a large component of the literary experience and should not be ignored in classroom teaching. His notion of the 'interpretive community' is consonant with the practice of many teachers who stress collaborative exchange in their teaching of literature, and is taken up by Fish, another American critic whose recent work has focused increasingly on the role of readers in the making of meaning.

In Fish's view, the literary work does not exist independent of the reader. For him, it is the reader who makes sense, not the text. He asserts that the critic's task is to describe 'the structures of the reader's experience rather than any structures available on the page' (Fish, 1980, p. 152). He sees this task as involving an analysis of the reader's responses 'in relation to the words as they succeed one another in time' (1980, p. 27), a notion of reading that is certainly open to debate. Fish seems to be saying that the meaning of a literary work is made up by a reader's experience of that work, a position that continues to focus only on one side of the relationship between the reader and text.

Fish does deal with the question of how such personal meanings are authorized, and offers the argument of 'interpretive communities', two or more individuals who share interpretive strategies and therefore read the text in the way demanded by these strategies. Readers may respond in different ways at different times depending on whether they shift from one community to another. Membership in a particular community therefore implies a predisposition to bring certain interpretive strategies to a particular text. The interpretive strategies of a particular interpretive community are employed tacitly and are not necessarily made explicit as a set of rules. Such strategies and the membership of interpretive communities are continually tested and renegotiated by the readings of other interpretive communities. It follows, for instance, that a classroom (depending on what is being read and for what purposes) may constitute one or more interpretive communities, and extend as well to other classrooms in the larger community. One of the tasks of this book is to suggest some possible strategies for developing interpretive communities, leaving readers with the task of developing these notions further.

Holland, Bleich, and Fish represent three positions along a continuum that emphasizes the experience of the reader. At one extreme is Holland for whom the text is virtually neutral and the reader the sole determiner of meaning. Both Bleich and Fish, while emphasizing the experience of the reader, advance the notion of 'interpretive communities', not exactly for the same reasons, as a means by which such readings are shareable and objectifiable.

Between texts and readers

This section is intended to suggest the aspect of reader-response theory that does not focus solely on the text or the reader but on what occurs in the transaction between the two. The best known proponents of this position are Iser and Rosenblatt. Let us outline first Iser's view as it is presented in his book, *The Act of Reading: A Theory of Aesthetic Response* (1978).

Iser argues that 'effects and responses are properties neither of the text nor of the reader; the text represents a potential effect that is realized in the reading process.' (Iser, 1978, p. ix). The text represents potential, a set of 'instructions' that wait to be activated by the reader. 'As the reader passes through the various perspectives offered by the text and relates the different views and patterns to one another he sets the work in motion, and so sets himself in motion, too' (Iser, 1978, p. 21). Reading is thus a process of *assembling* meaning. The reader is enabled and expected to inhabit the text as its co-author and to be aware of and hence evaluate the experience.

Iser's position differs from the reader-response critics we have discussed thus far in that he does not see the text as being neutral or inert but as incorporating two major interacting components. One is a latent 'repertoire' of social and cultural norms, elements and traditions of past literature. The other is a compendium of procedures or strategies to help the reader in reading the text (Iser, 1978, p. 69). Such a notion of text implies a reader who

> embodies all those predispositions necessary for a literary work to exercise its effect – predispositions laid down, not by an empirical outside reality, but by the text itself . . . the concept of the implied reader designates a network of response-inviting structures, which impel the reader to grasp the text (Iser, 1978, p. 34).

The concept of 'implied reader' does not assume a meaning fully determined by the text; Iser speaks of 'blanks', 'gaps' and 'indeterminacies' in the text which the reader must fill in:

Whenever the reader bridges the gaps, communication begins. The gaps function as a kind of pivot on which the whole text-reader relationship revolves. Hence the structured blanks of the text stimulate the process of ideation to be performed by the reader on terms set by the text (1978, p. 169).

Thus for Iser meaning is neither entirely subjective (the reader is directed by the formal properties of the text) nor completely controlled by the text (because of the reader's 'gap-filling' activity in constituting the text). Such a brief account does not fully represent Iser's carefully argued theory of 'aesthetic reading'. What is important for us is that by its hypotheses about the activities of readers and the ways in which literary texts 'direct' such activities, we are left with a picture of literary reading as a far more dynamic and unfinalized activity than we might assume from the ways literature has been traditionally taught.

Rosenblatt is another theorist who examines literary reading as a transaction between reader and text. In fact 'transaction' is a term she has used specifically to label this relationship and to displace 'interaction', the term more commonly used and in her eyes, one that misrepresents the relationship.

The 'transactional' terminology developed by John Dewey and Arthur F. Bentley seems most appropriate for the view of the demands of the reading process that I have attempted to suggest. . . . Dewey and Bentley sought to counteract the dualistic phrasing of phenomena as an 'interaction' between different factors, because it implies separate, self-contained, and already defined entities acting on one another – in the manner . . . of billiard balls colliding.
   . . . 'Transaction' designates, then, an ongoing process in which the elements or factors are, one might say, aspects of a total situation, each conditioned by and conditioning the other (1978, pp. 16–17).

The reader, the text and the event called the 'poem' are the three elements that are in a transactional relationship in Rosenblatt's theory of literary reading. Thus

The reading of a text is an event occurring at a particular time in a particular environment at a particular moment in the life history of the reader. The transaction will involve not only the past experience but also the present state and present interests or preoccupations of the reader. This suggests the possibility that printed marks on a page may even become different linguistic symbols by virtue of transactions with different readers. Just as a knowing is the process linking knower and a known, so a poem should not be thought of as an object, an entity, but rather as an active process lived through during the relationship between a reader and a text . . . it should not be confused with an object in the sense of an entity existing apart from author or reader (Rosenblatt, 1978, pp. 20–1).

By comparison with Iser and Rosenblatt, the positions advanced thus far seem to emphasize one or the other element (reader or text) at the expense of the other. Even where both elements seem to be equally considered as in Iser, there may still be a feeling of a slight domination by the text as it 'stimulates' the reader on its terms. Rosenblatt comes close to a model of literary reading that allows for a variety of readings and reading at different times and in different contexts, and by readers of different ages. Her drawing our attention to the contexts of reading is important, particularly when we consider that most of the reader-response critics we have cited thus far write as though people read literature in a vacuum or in a generalized kind of academic setting. In this regard, Rosenblatt makes a particularly useful distinction between aesthetic reading and what she calls 'efferent' reading:

> As the reader responds to the printed words or symbols, his attention is directed outward, so to speak, toward concepts to be retained, ideas to be tested, actions to be performed after the reading.
>
> To designate this type of reading, in which the primary concern of the reader is with what he will carry away from the reading, I have chosen the term 'efferent', derived from the Latin, 'efferre', to carry away. . . .
>
> In aesthetic reading, in contrast, the reader's primary concern is with what happens *during* the actual reading event. Though, like the efferent reader of a law text, say, the reader of Frost's 'Birches' must decipher the images or concepts or assertions that the words point to, he also pays attention to the associations, feelings, attitudes, and ideas that these words and their referents arouse within him. 'Listening to' himself, he synthesizes these elements into a meaningful structure. *In aesthetic reading, the reader's attention is centered directly on what he is living through during his relationship with that particular text* (pp. 24–5).

In drawing our attention to the two stances a reader may adopt, Rosenblatt makes clear that the same text may be read either efferently or aesthetically. It is worth reflecting how often school contexts unwittingly demand that pupils adopt an efferent stance towards literary texts.

Our review of reader-response theory was intended to make clear that reader-response critics, while stressing the role of the reader, are not in agreement as to what constitutes literary meaning and how that meaning is constituted. But they have raised important questions and these are not questions that are merely academic in their import. It matters for our teaching whether we are convinced that texts direct readers (as Todorov (1980, p. 77) puts it: 'A text always contains within itself directions for its own consumption') or if we believe that meaning is located exclusively in readers or in the transaction between reader and text. As all good questions, they need not confound us; in continuing to ask them we are less likely to settle into the model of classroom teaching where literary text is the sole repository of meaning and readers are but uninformed apprentices.

When it comes to revising teaching approaches, teachers are justifiably cautious. As a profession, we are concerned for our pupils, are jealous for the well-being of our craft, and are aware of what has worked well thus far. The changes in literary theory over the last five decades or so show a development in which attention has shifted from text to readers, and from reading the poem as a defined product to its being considered as a process. Our intention has been to suggest a possible progression which points towards the review of current practices, their adjustment and development. The convincingness of this line of development and our defence against being accused of faddishness lies in the fact that these new bearings have the support of current developments in reading theory, discourse studies, and research on reader-response. The following chapter looks at what could be called broadly the fields of reading theory and discourse analysis, fields which in the past have not been as closely associated with literary reading as they might have been.

2 Reading poetry

The major difference between Reader Response studies and studies in reading is one of scope: Reading Studies are far more comprehensive in defining their domain, taking in the reading of all varieties of text, while Reader Response studies are concerned exclusively with literary reading. There are as well significant differences in approach and emphasis. The prime focus of inquiries in Reading has been on understanding how skilled and unskilled readers read so that pupils can be taught to read. Thus Reading theorists and researchers have tended to concentrate on beginners and how they learn to read; they have shown little or no interest in literary reading. When they have attended to the efforts of older readers, they have dealt generally with initial encounters with text rather than with the extended, more comprehensive acts of interpretation that have been the preoccupation of Reader Response critics.

Reader Response critics have generally taken the text as read and focused more on the interpretations that have emerged. An important difference between Reading Studies and reader–response studies arises from the fact that, while Reader Response critics work primarily from their own informed readings of literary text, Reading researchers derive their data from the activities of readers representing a wide range of competencies in reading.

It is because they are concerned primarily with the process rather than with the products of reading that we need to consider at some length the contributions of researchers and theorists in the field of Reading. As was pointed out in Chapter 1, literary critical theory seems hardly to have been informed by the considerable amount of work that has gone on in Reading. We include in Reading that area of inquiry known as discourse processing, an area that has been defined in various ways. In this chapter, discourse processing is understood as an area of study which uses linguistic analysis to determine how written texts, usually short, are comprehended. While Reading theory and research have their primary roots in cognitive psychology, discourse analysis may be said to be an extension of psycholinguistics, sociolinguistics and descriptive linguistics. In the discussion that follows discourse processing studies are subsumed under the heading of Reading theory and research.

Until the 1960s, reading was largely regarded as a series of skills that exist in a hierarchical sequence, skills ranging from the basic decoding of the components of text to the more complex inferring of meaning. Meaning was regarded as residing entirely in the text and reading was a matter of deriving it through a process of decoding from what was on the page. Developments over the last decade have accelerated the recognition of the central role of the reader in the making of meaning and the consideration of reading as dealing with larger elements of text than phonemes, morphemes, words, phrases and sentences.

One difficulty in researching reading, and reading comprehension in particular, is that the process of reading does not issue in a visible product as writing does. To get at how readers process text, researchers have used a variety of experimental procedures, such as having subjects recall a passage they have read or answer questions about what they have read. One of the major problems with studies of comprehension, a problem that may have some bearing on the seeming irrelevance of most such research to literary reading, is that the texts used in such experiments are usually non-literary and, more often than not, specially written for the experiment. Moreover, they are fairly short and read in laboratory type situations which are hardly like the situations in which most people read.

Despite such criticisms, recent developments in Reading theory and research provide useful insights on the process of reading literature. These developments view reading largely as a process involving a dynamic interrelationship of a trinity: reader, text and situation. We have chosen to speak of these developments only inasmuch as they apply to the reading of poetry, and present a highly selective account under three overlapping headings:

1 The reader,
2 Reading poetic text,
3 The contexts of reading.

The reader

This section refers to those developments in Reading theory which describe how readers approach text and how readers' background knowledge is activated during reading. Reading theorists have proposed various models of the process by which readers come to understanding.

Bottom-up reading

One such model is described as 'bottom-up', a process by which readers attempt to compose an overall meaning by working up from the meanings of individual words and sentences to the larger units that contain these words and sentences. Accounts of bottom-up reading vary. Some theorists see readers as proceeding serially, decoding letters and words, applying syntactic and semantic rules to these words in order to arrive at sentences, comprehension and meaning. Others see some of the lower stages as having become largely automatic: that is, more proficient readers do not consciously attend to the shapes of letters and words, and rely to some extent on their own prior knowledge in working towards meaning. The reader who is preoccupied with understanding a poem sentence by sentence or line by line is making obstructions to progress in creating provisional understanding of the poem as a whole. At worst, extreme focus on an itemized reading may prevent *any* attention to the poem as poem.

Top-down reading

Prior knowledge, intentions and specific concepts affect the way in which a top-down reader operates. Working from such directional guidelines, top-down readers are inclined to 'sample' the text, developing and confirming hypotheses that account for various features of the text. Goodman (1967) speaks of reading as a psycholinguistic guessing game; and for similar reasons, Smith (1978) describes the reader as an interrogator of the text. As meaning emerges, top-down readers are likely to attend to specific words or phrases only if they find these words or phrases difficult to accommodate within their working hypotheses.

What might such processes look like? Consider, for instance, how some readers might proceed initially with Blake's 'The Sick Rose':

The Sick Rose

O Rose, thou art sick.
The invisible worm
That flies in the night
In the howling storm

Has found out thy bed
Of crimson joy,
And his dark secret love
Does thy life destroy.

Poems present particular difficulties to readers who tend to proceed bottom-up. As they decode in serial order and seem not to glance far enough ahead to gather the context within which the words they are reading occur, they usually work with meanings that are not necessarily borne out in the lines that follow. In many cases, they misperceive individual words because the appearances of these words and the meanings they suggest are not easily accommodated within the meaning they are deriving serially. Most beginning readers of poetry, even though they have read the title, will quite likely begin by assuming that the poem is about a person named Rose who is sick. But even adolescent readers, proceeding bottom-up, may or may not attend to the title. If they do, they may settle too soon on the idea that the poem is about a rose that is diseased, the victim of a worm that has been transported by a strong wind. As they read on, 'night', 'bed', 'crimson' and 'dark secret love' are likely to evoke images and feelings that seem out of place and inconsistent with such a reading, leaving them puzzled and frustrated and saying: 'Most poems do not make sense anyway.'

Top-down readers bring knowledge with them and expect to use it. The interaction between this knowledge and their first glancing at the poem produces an initial perspective which is likely to affect at least the early readings and understandings. Thus they may settle or not settle immediately on whether the rose addressed is a person or not and read the text accordingly. Top-down readers are also likely to hold both possibilities in mind and generate a hypothesis from the clues that follow that will accommodate one of those possibilities or define another. The point is that they will rely largely on their experience beyond the text to predict which developing sense best fits the knowledge they bring to it. Such readers, for instance, alerted by the likely metaphorical force of words like 'bed' and 'crimson joy' and confirmed in that notion by 'dark secret love' will probably reconsider their reading of 'the invisible worm' and the 'sickness' that has struck the rose.

Interactive reading

Interactive models of reading generally describe a process whereby the reader generates initial hypotheses about what the text is likely to mean and proceeds to test these in terms of the information provided by the text. In other words, there is a continuing to and fro movement from hypotheses to text. One might say the reader proceeds both bottom-up and top-down! The argument for an interactive model is that all means of processing and all kinds of information cooperate to produce meaning: in one instance particular words or phrases may suggest the revision of a hypothesis; in another, the reader's experience or recall of other texts may provide confirming evidence for how a particular phrase should be read; in still another, the recognition of the text as a poem may suggest that certain words are not to be taken literally. That 'The Sick Rose' is a poem alerts most readers to the probability that the 'worm that flies in the night' is no ordinary garden pest, an understanding that is reinforced by the appearance of 'bed of crimson joy' and 'dark secret love'. Any revision of the reader's original hypothesis leads to further readings in order to develop and test the revision and produce yet further revised hypotheses. There is no sense of absolute closure.

Schemata

Both top–down and interactive models of reading assign considerable weight to the reader's prior knowledge in the making of meaning. There has been much discussion as to how such prior knowledge is represented and activated during reading. A predominant notion derives from the work of Bartlett (1932) and his work on constructive processes in remembering. He proposed the notion of schemata for the mental frameworks his subjects constructed to retain a mental representation of a tale. Such schemata incorporated not only information from the story but elements from their experiences of other such stories as well. Schema Theory has since developed to posit the background knowledge 'activated' when readers encounter a particular text so that certain expectations as to what they are about to read or hear are set in motion. Thus the announcement that they are going to read a ballad should activate a ballad schema, a mental framework that will influence how that text is comprehended. Obviously ballad schemata vary for each individual and are continually modified and confirmed with each new instance of a ballad. According to van Dijk and Kintsch (1983):

> . . . schemata not only provide a coherent framework for the semantic units of a text, they also provide a basis for a more active, top–down process. Missing information can be assigned default values if it appears insignificant, or it can actively be looked for in the text. Deviations from the schema either may be accepted and registered, or, if they appear to be major ones, may become the basis for a problem-solving effort to try to account for them (p. 48).

There have been other notions advanced to help explain how background knowledge is activated during the process of reading. As the use of 'default' in the quotation above may suggest, some of these developments come from information processing theories and the work of computer scientists in Artificial Intelligence. Two of the better known concepts from Artificial Intelligence (AI) are *frames* and *scripts*.

Frames

There is obviously an overlap between the notions of 'schema' and 'frame'. Schemata represent structures of background knowledge that help us predict what we might expect from a particular text and therefore allow us to organize various elements of that text. With respect to poetry, frames may be understood as being less dynamic and far less comprehensive than schemata.

A frame, as defined by Minsky (1975), is 'a remembered framework to be adapted to fit reality by changing details as necessary'. Dillon (1980) speaks of frames as 'conceptual configurations' that help us integrate material in a text. For our purposes, 'frame theory' is useful because it suggests how some readers of poetry can manage to establish an appropriate fit for a particular word or situation in the poem or find the particular details in the poem that apply to the frame they have called up and others cannot. Frame theory also helps account for differences among individual interpretations and the difficulties many readers encounter. A word or phrase may suggest a frame that does not accord fully with other aspects of the poem. For a Canadian reader, the phrase 'mosquito-doped' (in 'Cyclops', a poem by Margaret Atwood) suggests someone covered in mosquito repellent and obviously prepared to spend some time outdoors in a landscape familiar to most Canadians (Frame 1). For most British readers, such a phrase inevitably conjures up an explorer somewhere in South America or Equatorial Africa (Frame 2). Most often when a word or phrase does activate an inappropriate frame, the reader either admits a failure to understand or works to redefine the details of the poem so that they will accommodate the frame.

Neither frames nor schemata are properties of texts. It is readers who bring *their* schemata to the text as active instruments of interpretation. We stress the active aspect because schemata are often misunderstood as templates applied mechanically to the text. As readers grow in experience of poetry, for instance, their store of schemata (e.g. modern and ancient ballads, folk songs, spirituals, pop lyrics) helps them read with increasing discrimination in the genre of popular poetry. But schemata are not limited to stored representations of literary text genres; readers rely on schemata that help them make sense of a train timetable and read that differently from how they would a stock market report. It is not only their particular discourse characteristics that figure in different schemata; each schema is inextricably meshed with and builds on the reader's past experiences with such discourse and related events.

Scripts

Reading and discourse processing theory have been reviewed in order to explore two key facets: (1) what expectations readers bring to the act of reading and (2) how readers' background knowledge, according to this theory, is activated in the reading process. A third notion arising from work on AI (Schank and Abelson, 1977) seeks to explain how background knowledge is stored and activated in reading through the use of 'scripts'. Scripts represent stereotypical sequences of actions in such events as going to the doctor or ordering a meal in a restaurant. Thus readers who are using a 'restaurant script' will know that what normally follows the waiter's approach and presentation of menus is not the customer's prompt request for the bill. The expectations of what will occur are likely to alter if the customer is rushing for a quick meal at the corner sandwich counter. Scripts differ from frames. Frames represent a standard set of *facts* about an object or a situation, whereas scripts represent a stereotyped sequence of *events*. The notion of scripts is helpful primarily because it partly explains how during reading, expectations are set up about what might normally follow in a situation, or how texts can rely on readers to infer what is not explicitly stated.

Because poetry invites considerable inferencing on the part of readers, they will often activate scripts that turn out to be inappropriate, given other details in the text. This is very much apparent in parts of the readings of Ted Hughes' 'The Thought-Fox' which are reproduced in Chapter 4. These readings will show also how some readers will replace a particular script or frame when its application turns out to be inconsistent with some of the details in the text.

This account of schemata, frames and scripts represents some of the considerable discussion that has grown around the issues of how readers' knowledge is called upon during reading. The theories that have been presented can only be reasonable approximations of what actually occurs in the complex transaction between reader and text. As was stated earlier, these theories have been posited on the basis of experiments with fairly short and specially written texts read in laboratory-type situations. They leave several questions unresolved. For instance, how are relevant schemata activated? What happens when a word or phrase activates several related frames? How does the reader select from among multiple variations of frames (or scripts)?

Because of its prime derivation from AI theory, such questions indicate that schema and related theory invite considerations that are fairly mechanical in their orientation. Such questions are not answered within the contexts of the short, artificial texts devised for such studies. Neither can they be answered in any satisfying way when applied to the complex experience of literary reading. As Spiro (1982) argues, schema theory fails to account for the experiential and qualitative aspects of literary reading, particularly for how we experience and reflect upon our initial *experience* of the poem, or how we comprehend and respond to our own comprehension of the poem.

Such work will go on; already, what were rather neat and precise definitions (for the purposes of AI studies) have softened somewhat to take account of their need to be sensitive to contexts (a discussion in van Dijk and Kintsch, 1983, pp. 310–11, is particularly useful here). This summary has set out to suggest that reading and discourse processing studies provide reasonable explanations and some empirical evidence in support of the reader-response critics' advocacy of the central role of readers in literary reading. There are of course other explanations that reading and discourse processing studies are continuing to provide in support of the current emphases in reader-response theory.

Inferencing

Thus far, this chapter has discussed various approaches readers might take in their transactions with literary text and examined some ways in which readers' knowledge is activated in literary reading. There are still other aspects of readers' relationships with literary text that remain to be considered and which continue to support the notion of readers as active makers of meaning. Foremost among these aspects of reading is *inferencing*, a term that refers to the process by which readers fill in missing links in the text using their own background knowledge to compose a coherent and sensible account of the text. In other words, readers begin with a sketchy model of the text based on two elements: what they encounter initially in the text, and the particular schema, frame or script activated. They go on progressively to fill in details or revise the model as they attempt to conform to the constraints and opportunities created by these elements. With growing familiarity with particular types of texts (e.g. recipes) some of the inferences readers are required to make become increasingly automatic; that is, readers come to such texts with set expectations, which are modified only when contrary information is encountered. In computer language this would be the 'default mode', which means: take these expectations as given unless instructed otherwise.

A quick glance through a cookbook will reveal how dependent its writers are on their readers making several inferences; for instance, if a cup of water is to be added, it is assumed that it will be cold or at room temperature. Instructions are also presented in a certain order without explicitly stating that the first instruction on the list has to be performed first, and so on. With a little experience, most readers of recipes are able to follow instructions fairly closely as they were intended by their writers. If they come to grief, it is usually because they are using an inappropriate schema or frame, they infer more than was intended or, what is more likely, proceed as though they are in familiar territory and skim through vital details.

Poems are far less explicit than recipes in setting forth how they must be read. They rely on readers' familiarity with the genre of poetry and its accompanying conventions; they count on the reader's active collaboration and expect that the connotative force of the language they use will help the reader evoke the images and experiences that are relevant; they depend on the reader's tolerance of uncertainty and an unwillingness to settle too easily and too soon on the framing structure that appears appropriate. As was argued in Chapter 1, what is unstated is just as much a part of the poem's meaning as what is stated; thus a reader's tolerance of ambiguity will to a great extent determine how he or she proceeds to *complete* the poem.

Consider, for instance, the opening lines of Ted Hughes' 'The Thought-

Fox' and some of the inferences which are typical of adolescent readers in coping with these opening lines:

> I imagine this midnight moment's forest:
> Something else is alive
> Beside the clock's loneliness
> And this blank page where my fingers move.
>
> Through the window I see no star:

Most readers of secondary school age will not have caught, at least at first reading, the force of the colon at the end of the first line and the implication that what follows the colon represents what the poem's 'I' imagines. (One difficulty is that once we have read through the poem, we cannot conceive with any degree of certainty how information from the poem was first taken in.) The force of that colon is not a given; it is most likely inferred retrospectively from what happens further in the poem. Another likely inference is an assumption of an identity between the 'I' in the poem and the poet himself. 'Midnight moment's forest' may introduce a note of foreboding for some readers (given the frame or script that such a phrase calls up), especially when it is combined with the notion of something else being *alive*, the clock's loneliness, and the starless night. A few readers will decide that the speaker is writing on the blank page, though they might be puzzled as to why the poet phrases it the way he does. Others will prefer to wait until they have found further evidence for such an inference. Some readers might hold tentatively that the speaker is blind and reading in braille. One group of pupils held that the speaker lived in the city 'because in the city you see no stars'.

Thus the text is construed partially through the first run, leaving gaps to be filled in and choices to be settled as one hypothesis or another is confirmed or rejected. Because the text is a poem and therefore brief enough to be rescanned at a glance, there can be a constant going back and forth in order to establish the shape of what is being presented. Thus, of the readers who feel the speaker is blind, some may hesitate and even revise this notion when they encounter: 'Through the window I see no star'; others may not notice this new information as bringing into question the speaker's apparent blindness; still others may sense the contradiction and yet leave it unresolved, especially if they have fixed on the idea that the speaker's moving finger indicates braille and blindness. For them, inference has become unshakeable fact and all other aspects of the poem must somehow fit or be ignored as somehow not making sense.

Rescanning of long prose texts is much less feasible. It is impossible for a reader of a novel to hold on to all the details with the same efficiency as a reader of a briefer text, a poem of conventional length. The novel will need to set up extensive and early cues, so that inferences can be established sooner and with greater certainty for the longer reading journey ahead. Cues will also need to be repeated in various ways – what reading theorists call 'redundant cueing' – in order to support the memory and retain and develop the inferencing necessary for interpretation of the story. Often writers will deliberately exploit such inferencing capabilities of readers in order to intrigue them. One popular example would be the labyrinths and surprise endings of most mystery novels. Readers who bring a mystery novel schema to such a text are more likely to enjoy collaborating with its setting-up than those who have not yet created such a schema.

Non-literary prose texts tend to rely much more on structural features to guide readers and control the reading. Headings and sub-headings, summary overviews, and the placement of key statements at the beginning rather than in the middle of paragraphs are some of the techniques employed in guiding and controlling the inferences readers might make and therefore ensuring that most readers arrive at roughly the same interpretation. We might recall here Rosenblatt's (1978) notion of aesthetic and efferent readings as descriptive of the stances readers are expected to take in approaching literary and non-literary texts respectively. 'Literary texts' obviously invite and encourage a kind of inferencing that is seldom appropriate in reading 'non-literary text'. Literary reading invites an openness to possibilities of meaning and a tolerance of ambiguity, ways of reading that often are counterproductive in reading non-literary text. Moreover, reading poetry relies on successive readings during which the experience of the poem is more fully evoked and created, making demands on Rosenblatt's aesthetic stance. Evidence suggests that many adolescents will bring an efferent stance to the reading of poetry and are quite frustrated by their failure to gain more than a cursory understanding.

We must glance back to 1929 and Richards' pioneering study on the responses to poetry of Cambridge University undergraduates in order to appreciate how the reading theory discussed thus far can provide an illuminating gloss of our understanding of literary reading. Richards listed 'ten chief difficulties of criticism', ten categories of failure in reading poetry (pp. 12–15). At least two of these difficulties may be understood in terms of the reading theory discussed in this chapter.

Richards speaks of 'mnemonic irrelevances' which are the 'misleading effects of the reader's being reminded of some personal scene or adventure, erratic associations, the interference of emotional reverberations from a past which may have nothing to do with the poem'. Richards also cites as another major difficulty stock responses which occur 'whenever a poem seems to, or does, involve views and emotions already fully prepared in the reader's mind, so that what happens appears to be more of the reader's doing than the poet's'. Reading theorists would speak of both these difficulties as instances of inappropriate schemata, scripts or frames being applied in attempts to work out an understanding of the poem. When Richards suggests that what happens may be more of the reader's doing than the poet's, he is obviously recognizing the readers' role (in Richards' view, disproportionate) in the making of the poem. In terms of reading theory, such readers fail to take sufficient account of the textual constraints that control interpretation, though we must admit that in poetic texts such constraints are often far less confining and directive than they are in non-literary texts.

Readers' expectations and intentions

This summary of developments in reading theory that have direct bearing on the reading of poetry has dealt primarily with the processes involved in comprehension. Clearly, such processes are directed by the expectations and intentions readers bring to texts, such as Rosenblatt's notion of reading for aesthetic and for efferent purposes.

Moreover, literary reading is not a two-tiered process where an efferent reading for what Richards has called 'plain sense' is topped-off by an aesthetic response. Rosenblatt insists literary reading occurs along a continuum between the two poles of aesthetic and efferent reading. At times during a reading efferent concerns may dominate (in reading a poem for a test, for instance); at others, a reading may be predominantly aesthetic, with the reader immersed in 'the lived-through experience of the work' (to use Rosenblatt's phrase). Whether the reading of a poem veers towards the efferent or the aesthetic depends on the expectations and intentions the readers bring to poetry.

Readers' expectations and intentions have other consequences as well. A sad but common fact is that many adolescent readers approach poetry with the expectation that they can make little or no sense of a poem on their own. Such expectations are inevitably self-fulfilling prophecies; like us, they read differently when they do not expect to understand a text, tending to read bottom-up rather than top-down, expecting that a careful working out of the meaning at the sentence level will somehow help to break the code. This preoccupation with local detail defeats any attention to experiences the poem might evoke. In fact, such readers may well distrust such evocations; especially if, in the past, they have seemed irrelevant in the light of what has generally been proposed by the teacher as 'the meaning' of the poem.

It should be made clear that most expectations and intentions operate automatically, below the level of conscious awareness; unless of course they are somehow frustrated. Culler (1975), for instance, suggests that readers adopt 'a rule of significance': they assume that the writer will attempt to say something significant about the human condition. Such an automatic assumption can lead to readers saying they have not understood a poem when they actually mean they have been unable to realize any significance from the poem. Readers also tend to 'favour' information in the poem that fits in with their expectations of the poem's meaning and 'ignore' information that does not obviously fit the meaning they are creating. Another automatic expectation for many readers of poetry is that they are reading a fiction; and that fictions are likely to be more preoccupied with truths than with facts.

The act of reading a poem can also be affected by past experiences of how poems have been variously read and dealt with in school. One's attitudes to reading poetry are inextricably part of a reading history, a history of successes and failures that determine one's expectations of a poem, how one goes about reading and making sense of a poem, and the purposes one reads for. If the teaching of prosody has been the focus of instruction, pupils are likely to read a poem in order to talk about its formal features, such as the arrangement of lines, rhyming schemes, meter, and hidden figures of speech. If the teacher has treated the pupils as partners in a conversation with the poem which involves all of them, pupils are likely to read the poem with some confidence in their resources as readers. If poems have been read as though meaning resided entirely in the text, pupils are likely to believe it is their task somehow to ferret it out. If classroom teaching has encouraged a view of poetry as something with a meaning stubbornly hidden in the text and revealed only to the fortunate few, many readers are likely to do no more than engage in making probing guesses, hoping that somehow the poem's meaning will occur to them.

Such a view of reading derives from an outdated mechanistic model of language which sees the act of communication as a process of 'shunting' information from sender to receiver (Smith, 1985, p. 195). The poem communicates its meaning, the reader receives. We would argue along with Rosenblatt and Smith for a more creative role for the reader of poetry. Such a role authorizes readers' bringing their own knowledge, experience and sensibilities to *their* reading. That knowledge should include experiences of other texts as well, or as Barthes puts it, the 'plurality of other texts' which make up the 'I' of the reader (Barthes, 1974).

There is increasing support in current reading theory for this principle of authorizing readers. One particularly important concept is the notion of metacognitive awareness, readers' awareness of their own reading strategies and an ability to monitor and regulate their own processes as readers. When reading poetry, such awareness allows them to determine whether their hypotheses account adequately for what the text offers, what words or phrases remain intractable in terms of the hypotheses they are working with, and overall, whether their reading makes sense. Classroom practices in teaching poetry can either encourage or discourage the growth of these self-monitoring strategies. Encouraging pupils to exercise their autonomy as readers and be more fully accountable for their readings can only help to foster such growth. This will be a major theme in the ensuing chapters.

Reading poetic text

In Chapter 1 it was pointed out that a major orientation in reader-response criticism was towards examining how texts *acted* on readers or were blueprints for readers' responses. Such a literary critical concern has its counterpart in Reading theory which examines how texts are structured and hence direct the cognitive processes by which readers comprehend them. Such an approach to studying reading processes differs from that which considers that the reader has some part to play if only through the activation of prior knowledge in the form of stored representations such as schemata, scripts and frames. Here the focus instead is on the reading process as it is represented in the text.

As with most such studies in reading, text processing studies have focused almost entirely on relatively short prose passages. Where short narrative passages have been used, they have more often than not been specially written for the purpose. As was pointed out earlier, such studies seem unworkable with texts that invite an aesthetic stance. What insights then can be gained from such studies that would help explain the relationships between readers and poetic texts?

In the most general terms, such studies are concerned to discover how meaning is presented in text so that it is recoverable in the act of reading. One might examine a poem, for instance, to determine what particular features make that text coherent. Halliday and Hasan's *Cohesion in English* (1976) has been a good starting point for many such studies of prose passages. Certain stylistic features alert readers to a particular kind of discourse: the opening lines of Shakespeare's Sonnet CXVI, 'Let me not to the marriage of true minds/Admit impediments . . .' suggests the beginning of an argument; whereas, 'Late August, given heavy rain and sun . . .' (in Heaney's 'Blackberry-Picking') is more likely the opening of a narrative. Text structures also vary in the order in which information is presented, in the differences of levels of generalization, in whether high-order generalizations derive from or precede low-level ones, in the number and kinds of propositions that are implicit in the text, and in how they are supported and developed. Such structures are obviously supportive of or disallow particular inferences on the part of the reader and should therefore not be considered apart from the reader's own processing strategies.

These instances are offered only to suggest some of the ways poetic text might be examined to determine the kinds of readings they make feasible and the kinds of difficulties that adolescent readers might fall into. Readers who wish to read more about discourse processing should consult van Dijk and Kintsch (1983) and Dillon (1978). Widdowson's *Stylistics and the Teaching of Literature* (1975) examines the linguistic and rhetorical structures of literary texts to demonstrate how meaning is represented in such texts.

An alternative strategy is to look at far more obvious instances of how texts direct comprehension, instances that do not rely on bringing complex discourse analyses procedures to poems. Thus we might consider the kinds of demands made on readers: What prior knowledge is assumed? How do syntax and word usage deviate from contemporary norms and present difficulties to readers? Several 13-year-olds reading the last two lines of Blake's 'The Poison Tree',

> In the morning glad I see
> My foe outstretch'd beneath the tree.

were hard put to decide whether the foe is dead or stretched out relaxing beneath the tree. Has there been a reconciliation between the foe and the speaker? And is it the speaker, the foe, or the morning that 'glad' applies to? Interestingly, the scenario a reader has begun to construct for this poem will to a large extent determine which choices occur to the reader. The scenario in turn will have been influenced by the hypothesis suggested by a combination of several cues from the text and the reader's prior knowledge. Here again is another illustration of the dynamic relationship between reader and text that Rosenblatt has called transactional.

Another alternative is to consider the possibilities offered by a poem in terms of the kinds of readings it *invites*. Tillyard (1945) distinguishes between direct poetry and oblique poetry: 'Briefly, the poetry of Direct Statement contains few if any references beyond those explicitly stated; the poetry of Oblique Statement is highly evocative and may imply emotions or ideas not explicitly stated.' A consequence of oblique statement is that the reader may not be sufficiently constrained by the text; on the other hand, direct statement allows the reader to take only what is stated and not feel the need to draw out what is implicit and felt. Such readings often occur with poems that are narrative in form, where because of easily accessible narrative schemata, the reader does not feel the need to go beyond what is directly stated. Lanham (1983, pp. 18–19) distinguishes between 'looking at' the text – a self-conscious reading for style, a concern for the verbal surface – and 'looking through' the text – reading only for information. Reading poetry usually involves a stance somewhere between 'looking at' and 'looking through'. This is not a fixed stance because as intentions, expectations, attitudes or attention shift, and as new recognitions arise, there will be corresponding movements towards one or the other mode of reading. It is quite likely as well that readers will lean towards one or the other stance as a consequence of particular characteristics of the poem. Some poems, the poems of e. e. cummings, for instance, invite an initial dwelling on the verbal surface; others – many of the poems of Robert Frost, for instance – initially draw readers to the events behind the words and the voice of the implied speaker. Generally, in the initial reading, readers will shift back and forth between the two stances. If they read poetry often enough, pupils should develop a flexibility that allows them to recognize and adapt to the particular invitations of each poem.

The contexts of reading

Thus far in our discussing Reading theory we have given most place to attempts to describe the complex role of the reader in action. The extent to which literary texts direct the processes by which readers comprehend texts has also been considered. More recently, the contexts in which such texts are read have come to be regarded as influencing considerably the transactions between readers and texts.

The influence of contexts is apparent in the first place in the intentions readers bring to literary text. *Why* people read determines to a large extent *how* they read. Such an understanding is implicit in Rosenblatt's description of the efferent and aesthetic stances readers adopt towards literary text. The intentions behind the act of reading literature as a familiar recreational and satisfying activity, with the option of choosing the time and place when one reads, are obviously not transferable to those classrooms where literature is read only to be studied. For most pupils reading poetry is very much a school-related activity. Unlike their experience of the reading of prose fiction, these pupils have little personal history of reading poetry to set against the reading they may do in school. School contexts determine largely what pupils conceive poetry to be and how they believe it is 'correct' to read it.

The initiators of those contexts have certain choices to make. One is whether to include or disvalue personal and private feeling from the act of reading poetry and reference to personal experience as a way of validating what is read. Where there is exclusion it is inevitably part of an assumption that meaning resides in the text, the text is the sole reference point for interpretation, and the arbiter of its meaning is the teacher, who is of course the most qualified reader (academically) in the classroom. Where these circumstances prevail, it is no wonder that most pupils feel insecure as readers of poetry and read accordingly, seeking to discover the one right meaning that is drawn out bit by bit through the teacher's questioning and, in the process, setting aside their own intuitions of what the poem might mean.

If as we have argued thus far, reading poetry calls for the active involvement of readers in the making of meaning rather than a passive receptiveness, then school contexts need to ensure that such interactive reading is made possible, and safeguarded and valued. Most social psychologists agree that reading is an adaptive response to the circumstances in which it occurs. Thus pupils who might read tentatively and with an openness to possibilities of meaning are at odds if they find themselves having to cope with approaches which imply that the correct answers are locked in the head of the teacher. As we hope to show in Chapter 5, there are many ways in which teachers assign authority to readers and ensure more responsible readings of poetry. Such approaches lie along the path of moving away from an information processing model that is implicit in some teaching of poetry, and all too often represented in comprehension exercises, towards assigning responsibility to readers for the meanings they make individually and as members of collaborative groups.

Reading and responsiveness

This chapter has attempted to show that there are aspects of Reading theory and research which have an important bearing on understanding how adolescents read poetry, even though much of the research reviewed derives primarily from studies based on the comprehension of non-literary prose. As a result, one of the major gaps in Reading theory has been the lack of sufficient regard to reading as experience or as Rosenblatt puts it, 'the lived through experience of the work'. The phrases, 'I feel', 'I sense', 'I imagine' seem out of place in Reading research, particularly since they refer to the experiences of readers and are not directly applicable to the text.

In his essay, 'In Search of Fundamental Values' (1964), Knights emphasizes the central importance of the experiential in reading poetry. He provides several arguments:

1 Thinking in reading poetry is primarily in terms of images, not in terms of abstract concepts. Such thinking is therefore in 'the fullest possible relation to the intimate personal life of the reader' (p. 78).
2 What is known in reading poetry is below the level of full consciousness; it is not known as an object existing independently of the reader. Thus 'knowledge of poetry – the knowledge that comes through poetry – demands not only an active but a relaxed and receptive mind' (pp. 78–9).
3 Knights also warns against too great a stress on conscious understanding: 'Poetry of any depth maybe intuitively apprehended before the experience can be critically defined . . . and even in the most concentrated act of attention to literature there is a quality of relaxed absorption that makes activity like rest.' (p. 81).

While Reading theory has helped inform our understanding of reading processes, Knights' concerns are an important reminder of the centrality of the unconscious and the intuitive in reading literary text. There is a tendency among Reading theorists to prescribe teaching practices that bring to conscious attention strategies for comprehension that are normally tacit and inexplicit. As a counter to such urgings we need constantly to keep in mind Langer's reminder that the 'entire qualification one must have for

understanding art is responsiveness' (1953, p. 396). How such responsiveness is engaged in reading literature has been the subject of considerable
research over the last two decades. Chapter 3 reviews the findings of such
research and considers their implications for teaching poetry.

3 Research on response to poetry: what we have learned

The preceding chapters considered how literary critical theory and reading and discourse processing theory might inform our understanding of what occurs in transactions between readers and poems. In this chapter we turn to the fairly comprehensive body of research on response to literature, to identify some developments that have particular relevance for the teaching of poetry.

Surveys of research on response to literature record a wide variety of work, particularly since the mid-1960s. Much of this work focuses on the role of readers as active interpreters of literary text and on the nature of the transaction between readers and 'poems'. Such studies are concerned variously with the process of responding itself, identifying elements of readers' responses to literature, factors involved in understanding literature and difficulties readers encounter, factors influencing readers' judgements of literature, and the relationship of a variety of elements such as age, sex, attitude, and the genre of the literary work. While these studies differ widely in methodology and significance, they in common deny the traditional status of the literary work as an autonomous object and reinforce the reader's role in the making of meaning. We have been quite selective in what we have chosen to report, confining ourselves to those findings we believe are likely to command assent not only because they are consistent with the theoretical position developed thus far, but also because they have clear implications for practice.

I. A. Richards' *Practical Criticism*

I. A. Richards' investigation of undergraduates' responses to poetry (*Practical Criticism*, 1929) is significant not only because it comes so early in the history of such studies and has since been an important guide to practice and further research, but also because it raises some issues that have continued to bedevil the teaching of poetry. One such issue is the traditional authority and respect accorded poetry and the consequent disvaluing of the experiences of readers. By withholding the names of the authors of poems which his students were asked to read and comment on over several readings, Richards realized how dependent his readers were on traditional interpretation and authority for the judgements they made. From his analyses of his readers' protocols Richards was also able to elaborate an argument for the several levels or aspects of meaning that operate in one's reading of a poem: levels of 'Sense, Feeling, Tone, and Intention' (p. 175), an argument that suggests that any consideration of the problem of 'making out the meaning' cannot ignore the fact that there are several kinds of meaning.

Another important contribution to an understanding of response is Richards' account of the 'principal obstacles and causes of failure in the reading and judgment of poetry' (p. 15). These ten difficulties are well worth reviewing, particularly because they focus entirely on the reader's role in the transaction.

1 The difficulty of making out the plain sense: 'readers of poetry frequently and repeatedly *fail to understand it* [poetry] both as statement and as an expression . . . and equally they misapprehend its feeling, its tone, and its intention' (p. 12). We might consider for our own practice how in our teaching we tend to concentrate on one aspect of meaning at the expense of others, and ignore the fact that some readers are likely to have keyed into the poem at the symbolic and affective level, while others are wrestling with 'plain sense'.

2 Difficulties of sensuous apprehension: the difficulty of sensing or perceiving the sounds and rhythms of the words (pp. 12–13). Readers with such difficulties might benefit from hearing poems read aloud as well as from being encouraged to experiment with reading aloud a poem in various ways.

3 Difficulties connected 'with the place of imagery, principally visual imagery': difficulties arising primarily from differences among individuals in their capacity to visualize (p. 13). Such differences are quite likely the source of serious differences among readers' apprehensions of a poem, differences that often make readers feel uncertain about their poetry-reading capabilities.

4 Mnemonic irrelevancies: 'the misleading effects of the reader's being reminded of some personal scene or adventure, the interference of emotional reverberations from a past which may have nothing to do with the poem' (p. 13). Of course, such reminders could be relevant as well; it would therefore be a serious constraining of the reader's role to discourage such personal associations.

5 Stock responses: 'views and emotions already fully prepared in the reader's mind. . . . What happens appears to be more of the reader's

doing than the poet's' (p. 14). In other words, the transaction between reader and text is too heavily weighted on the reader's side. Such triggering may be far too automatic for the reader to be aware of its occurring.

6 Sentimentality: 'over-facility in certain emotional directions' (p. 15). A response is sentimental 'if it is too great for the occasion' or if it is 'inappropriate to the situation that calls it forth' (pp. 244, 246).

7 Inhibition: while not necessarily bad in itself, what 'is unfortunate is the permanent curtailment of our possibilities as human beings, the blanking out, through repeated and maintained inhibition, of aspects of experience that our mental health requires us sometimes to envisage' (p. 253).

8 Doctrinal adhesions: views and beliefs about the world that bear upon the reader's estimate of the poetry – 'a fertile source of confusion and erratic judgment' (p. 14).

9 Technical presuppositions: judging 'poetry from outside by technical details' and thus 'putting means before ends' (p. 15).

10 General critical preconceptions: 'prior demands made upon poetry as a result of theories – conscious or unconscious – about its nature and value' (p. 15).

Richards believes these difficulties are not unconnected with one another and that they overlap. It may strike readers that some of these difficulties have their sources in some school practices and attitudes. These difficulties may also not be as readily apparent in the work of secondary pupils as they are in the university student protocols Richards cites, if only because secondary pupils are not likely to write at sufficient length to reveal the full range of difficulties they encounter as readers of poetry.

Overcoming difficulties in the reading of poetry

It is ironical that Richards' focusing on the difficulties of readers led to the New Critical emphasis on close reading, attempts to exclude the readers' concerns and attitudes and dwell exclusively in the text. The New Critical approach was primarily one of making the reading of literature impervious to subjective and contextual influences. There were, however, important attempts to understand readers' difficulties with poetry and suggest how they might be overcome. Two studies of particular interest are Britton's 'Evidence of Improvement in Poetic Judgment' (1954) and Harding's 'Practice at Liking: A Study in Experimental Aesthetics' (1968).

Britton found that readers' ability to discriminate between true and false poems ('false' poems were specially concocted for the study) improved when readers were re-tested four to six months later: although 'false' poems were preferred in the initial readings, preferences had converged towards the 'true' poems in the later re-readings. The results suggest that a growing familiarity with poetry is in itself a factor in the improvement of poetic judgement; that time spent reading poetry (not necessarily time spent in close and intensive study of a few poems) is a means of cultivating discrimination. 'The primary condition for its occurrence would seem to be that poetry should be read and returned to' (p. 206). Also worth noting is Britton's observation about the intervention in poetic judgement of the reader's preconceived ideas, attitudes and sentiments. He suggests that 'stock responses and other forms of prejudice may sometimes be adopted out of instinctive caution: a protective measure, so to speak, against the new experience where it is of an emotional kind; and a refuge instead in the familiar emotional situation preconceived' (p. 206).

Harding's study (1968) demonstrates that repeated readings of poems over a period of time, in this case four readings over a week, constitute practice at a task and lead to changes in evaluation of these poems. Thus over the four readings *an increasing proportion* of poems were rated as poems that were liked but were so easily understandable that they might not offer much more on further reading. A *decreasing proportion* of poems were judged too difficult but likely to be rewarding if read often enough and with care. In other words, increasing familiarity with poetry (without explicit instruction) over even a short period of time does lead to changes in judgement though not consensus – poems do become easier to comprehend and, more often than not, less attractive in terms of what a further reading might offer. Quite clearly, both Britton's and Harding's studies suggest that pupils need to be allowed time to grow familiar with poems before they are asked to describe and judge. Their findings also bring into question examination practices that allow pupils little opportunity to grow familiar with the poems they are invited to write about.

The elements of response to poetry

Both Britton and Harding used the stated preferences or judgements of their readers to identify changes in their readers' perceptions of particular poems over time. Their experiments did not call for fuller responses that might explain how their readers had arrived at their judgements. One of the major and more influential attempts to understand the responding process was undertaken by Purves and Rippere in their study, *Elements of Writing About a Literary Work* (1968). Drawing on a bank of critical statements by literary scholars and student essays, Purves and Rippere identified 139 elements that provided a means of analysing and categorizing the content of a reader's written response to a literary work and thereby a means of describing the processes involved in the formulation of a response. The units for analyses are the 'statements' that make up the written response.

The elements fall into four major categories:

1 *Engagement–involvement*: 'the various ways in which the writer [reader] indicates his surrender to the literary work' (p. 6), statements indicating liking or disliking the work, some form of emotional reaction to the work or to aspects of it.
2 *Perception*: 'encompasses the ways in which a person looks at the work as an object distinct from himself and . . . separate from the writer's [reader's] consideration of the world around the writer' (p. 6).
3 *Interpretation*: 'the attempt to find meaning in the work, to generalize about it, to draw inferences from it, to find analogues to it in the universe that the writer [reader] inhabits' (p. 7).
4 *Evaluation*: 'statements about why the writer [reader] thinks the work good or bad. His judgment may be derived from either a personal or an objective criterion' (p. 8).

Purves and Rippere argue that the elements are neutral, a means of analysis rather than assessment. Thus the elements are not meant to be considered hierarchically; nor are they exhaustive or taxonomical. Purves and Rippere believe other elements may appear as they examine more written responses, especially from cultures other than their own. Using these elements, researchers have been able to describe, for instance, particular emphases in responses and to consider the relationships of these responses to specific teaching approaches or to other factors such as sex, age or ability. A useful survey of research that has used these elements is provided by Applebee (1977).

Some of the more interesting and useful findings cited by Applebee are those that track age-related differences. Responses 'of pre-adolescent children focus primarily upon the category "perception" and the sub-category "content", shifting during adolescence toward a higher proportion of interpretation' (Applebee, 1977, p. 259). Such studies generally show that the range of responses increases with age, that there is a gradual shift from the literal aspects of a story, for instance, to interpretation, and that there is a concomitant decrease in engagement–involvement responses. Analyses of sex-related differences indicate largely that girls 'seem somewhat more willing than boys to verbalize engagement–involvement response, which may be a response to cultural expectations of appropriate "masculine" behavior' (Applebee, 1977, p. 259). Applebee also reports that 'differences in response preferences between stronger and weaker students are relatively minor, except as byproducts of difficulty in comprehending a work'. When pupils have difficulty in comprehending a work, they tend to shift from statements of interpretation to statements in the perception and content categories (Applebee, 1977, p. 259).

One of the more ambitious applications of the Purves–Rippere categories is a study of achievement in literature in ten countries (Purves, 1973). The study, sponsored by the International Association for the Evaluation of

Educational Achievement, developed several instruments 'to identify and measure important dimensions of aesthetic response' (p. 9) and to ensure a high degree of reliability in the process. In fact, the Purves–Rippere categories were developed primarily as a means towards establishing such reliable measures. One of the more important findings to emerge from the study is:

> Response to literature is a learned behavior. . . . It is modified by what the student reads and it is affected by his culture, and, presumably, by his school as an inculcator of that culture. Response to literature might be said to be a 'cognitive style', a way of thinking about literary experience, a way of ordering that thinking for discourse (p. 315).

If, as Purves and his colleagues conclude, 'schools seem to indoctrinate students into a pattern of response' (p. 315), we need to consider how school practices and policies might develop a climate that allows pupils to discover and exercise a higher degree of freedom in the ways they choose to respond.

One of the major problems with the Purves–Rippere content analysis scheme is that in its attempt to provide reliable empirical evidence and be descriptive rather than evaluative, it assigns equal weight to all statements in a response, weighing the particular character of a response by the preponderant categories in that response. Thus a central pivotal statement in one category can be assigned the same worth as a minor passing comment in another category. One might also question whether many statements in a reader's response are not implicitly evaluative: there is a valuing implicit in what one chooses to notice and not notice in a poem. And much of that choosing may have to do with the rhetorical context within which the response is reported rather than with the ways the writer has actually responded to the literary text. These problems are cited in order to point out a need for care in undertaking studies of response, a need to consider carefully the nature of the evidence that is cited and the extent to which such evidence is truly indicative of the process it claims to represent.

Oral responses to literature

Several of the studies Applebee cites in his review of research using the Purves–Rippere categories rely on oral responses for their primary data. Oral response one might argue is more directly and fully reflective of the responding process than written response. Much written response is what one might call 'secondary response', a response to a response. Even where researchers have asked readers to write freely in response to a literary text, there is always the suggestion that the act of writing somehow interposes itself between the response and one's articulation of that response. A study by Travers (1982) of a 14-year-old's oral response to a poem shows how without training he is able to 'explore most of the aspects of a poem which teachers would hope for, including the demand for evidence to support his views' (p. 57); however, what he is able to write or chooses to write falls far short of representing the fullness of his response to the poem.

Small-group discussion of poetry as a record of the dynamic process of responding is also a promising means of understanding response to poetry. There have been several classroom experiments with relatively undirected small-group discussion of literature, most of these to demonstrate the pedagogical effectiveness of such procedures and provide instances of learning through talk (Barnes *et al.*, 1971; Beach, 1972; Stratta *et al.*, 1973; Dixon, 1974; Mills, 1974; Torbe, 1974; Grugeon and Walden, 1978; Jackson, 1982). Because the agenda develops in discussion, such talk provides useful insights about how readers compose meaning together. We know, for instance, that many groups spend some time establishing the 'facts' or 'events' in the text, asking, in effect, whether they are all reading the same text. What is going on here? Who is doing what to whom? Too often large-group teaching proceeds as though the 'facts' are apparent to everyone who has read the text. If we consider Harding's (1937) and Britton's (1972) notions of 'spectatorship', we can understand how different readers enter discussion with differing versions of what is happening.

Case studies of response

With growing awareness of the variety of factors that impinge on the act of reading, increasing attention has been given to studying readers in context and over time. A model of such an investigation is Meek's (1983) study of adolescents learning to read, a narrative compiled from the work of six teachers. While the book is concerned primarily with the difficulties of adolescents who believe they cannot read, there are powerful lessons for all teachers who are concerned with how adolescents cope with the reading demands of school. One of the arguments of this book is that teachers need to know adolescents as individual readers, and that they should take fuller account of the contexts within which reading tasks are set. Meek's observations are quite pertinent in this respect:

> Our pupils learned to read when we made it seem worthwhile, and to the extent that we expected them to be able to. They learned best when, instead of grinding away at unfamiliar text with intermittent success, they *composed* the text. Then the roles were reversed; they were the authority for what was said and their frame of reference became the dominant one.

Even though Meek is referring to texts the pupils had written themselves, the notions of ownership and authority implied apply to the reading of poetry as well. Clearly contexts for reading poetry, particularly the role assumed by the teacher as someone who needs to be and can be informed, can make a crucial difference to how adolescents take on the task of reading poetry and the extent to which they succeed as readers.

Developing independent readers of poetry

The argument thus far has been that school contexts can often be inhospitable to the reading of poetry, and that the teacher's role as expert reader reinforces the conviction of many pupils that they cannot read and understand poems on their own. What will pupils accomplish as readers of poetry if they are trusted to read and apprehend poetry on their own? What follows is a description of an attempt to answer that question (Dias, 1979, 1987). That description is given at some length because this study and the one that follows represent attempts to answer some of the key questions that have arisen thus far, specifically, what are the real abilities of adolescents as readers of poetry? And how do we proceed in finding out about these abilities and taking account of them in classrooms?

Answers to these questions begin in the notion that the realization of a poem should involve a process whereby each pupil has the opportunity to confirm and develop his or her experience of the poem in a collaborative sharing of responses within a small group. Together the group try to articulate their understanding of the poem. That understanding will have to be shared with other groups in further collaborative exchange. The role of the teacher is that of active and interested listener, one who is curious about the understandings that will be reported, but not in any sense the expert who will provide the final answers to the 'puzzle' of the poem. Above all, the teacher communicates a conviction that each of the groups and the groups together have among themselves the resources to make sense of the poem for themselves. These notions translate into the following procedures.

Procedures

1 Groups are formed. A leader for each group is chosen with the responsibility for chairing the discussion and reporting the group's account of the poem. Group members are to take turns at chairing discussion sessions.
2 Copies of the poem are distributed. The teacher reads the poem.
3 A pupil reads the poem. The teacher determines from the reading probable sources of misunderstanding caused by syntax or unfamiliar words.
4 The teacher invites inquiries about meanings of unfamiliar words and assists without directing interpretation. Pupils are encouraged to respond to such inquiries; but this stage of dwelling on words even before the context has emerged is not drawn out.
5 Pupils read the poem aloud within their groups and then silently. Within the group, each pupil is expected to state *in turn* an initial reaction, feeling or observation occasioned by the readings. Pupils are not to

remark on one another's responses until each member of the group has shared an initial response. (This is an important stage in the process and is strictly followed. Some individuals cannot wait to confront others and, if they are articulate, overwhelm reticent members of the group, who are likely to forget what they were going to say.)

6 Following this preliminary round of comment, pupils are no longer required to speak in turn and may comment freely on what they have just heard and share observations in their endeavour to arrive at some sense of the poem. A means of keeping the discussion going is to have pupils read in turn a sentence or stanza at a time, commenting as they go along. This allows pupils to interrupt with comments and questions as they build up their sense of the poem. It also helps the group establish the text of the poem: what is and is not there in the text.

7 Any time an impasse is reached in discussion, the pupils are encouraged to return to the text of the poem.

8 Half-way through the discussion and also near the end of the group discussion, the pupils are encouraged to re-read the poem in the light of new realizations.

9 Near the end of the discussion, usually 20–25 minutes into the session, one member in each group re-reads the poem aloud; the members of the group take account of any meanings that have emerged and prepare an account that represents their experience of the poem, this account to be shared with the large group. At all times the teacher's concern is not to influence the form and content of this account.

  The large-group session usually involves pupils reporting in turn for their groups. After the first group has reported, the onus is on each subsequent reporter to build on the previous account, agreeing and disagreeing, and reporting any new insights that have occurred in the process. Members of the group supplement their reporter's accounts of the poem if they feel the need to and record minority opinions.

10 The several accounts of the poem should create the impression that the poem is much more than each of the summary accounts has made out. It remains for the teacher to raise questions that arise from the discussions and the groups' reports, to help relate some of the several strands in the groups' reports, to introduce where useful the terminology that helps the class make sense of and place their observations. During this 'wrap-up' the teacher should at all costs avoid creating the impression that the groups do not have the resources within themselves to deal adequately with the poem, and that the teacher is the ultimate repository of and arbiter of the poem's meaning. The questions that are raised by the teacher at this concluding stage must be real questions sparked by an interest in the inquiring of the pupils and reinforcing a belief in their own resources as readers.

  The procedure is structured but non-directive; it prescribes a procedure for inquiring into a poem, but does not direct the meaning that will be realized. The structure helps initiate pupils who are unused to group discussion into the procedure. It allows for the registering of initial responses, encourages frequent re-readings, and insists that members of groups and groups themselves listen to one another. Readers might wonder if the procedure focuses too much on 'making sense' at the expense of formal, affective and aesthetic concerns. Transcripts of the discussions do reveal, however, that aesthetic and formal concerns are touched on as the groups realize a greater confidence as readers, and the poem becomes less a puzzle and more an experience. Moreover, the small group setting allows pupils to draw on their personal experiences and express feelings without fear of embarrassment.

Results

In both the original study and its replication eight years later (Bryant, 1984) the results are remarkably similar. The pupils involved in the small-group procedure scored significantly higher in the post-test than did a control group of pupils of similar ability taught the same set of poems in a traditional large-group format. There were other gains as well:

1 In their daily journals the pupils reported a growing positive attitude towards poetry as well as increasing confidence in their ability to make sense of poetry on their own.
2 In the transcripts of group discussions there is clear evidence that the pupils formulate meaning tentatively, are less defensive about their own opinions, willing to listen to one another, and quite ready to turn to the text in order to confirm their observations.
3 There is a growing willingness to postpone closure, to live with ambiguity. There is some evidence that some groups value differences in interpretation when other groups report. Such differences remind them of the several possibilities of meaning that a poem represents.
4 Because the procedure allows so many pupils to speak so often, and to do so without risk, there is a noticeable improvement in pupils' abilities to voice what are quite often complex and subtle observations about what they have read.

To sum up, the value of this procedure lies in the positive interdependence, the notion of a collaborative community, that is built up throughout the process. Just as valuable is the responsibility accorded pupils for making meaning and the resulting confidence of the pupils in their own resources as readers. Above all, the study confirms that pupils accorded such responsibility realize a high level of competence as readers of poetry.

What happens when they read a poem

The small-group procedure described above is an effective means of helping pupils develop more fully their resources as readers of poetry. Transcripts of such discussions give some hints of how readers collaboratively create meaning, but the process appears to be largely one of chance intuitions and fortuitous turns of thought. Some readers appear to be more successful than others; other seemingly unsuccessful readers often make key observations. By what process do individuals arrive at the meanings they offer to the group? Even partial answers to that question might help teachers work towards ensuring that classroom practices are at least consonant with those processes and not indifferent to them or at worst at odds with them.

Little is known about what happens in transactions between readers and poems simply because much of what occurs remains tacit and unavailable to introspection or recall. Moreover, much of the data that has been used to discover what occurs has come from written or oral responses, in most cases retrospective accounts of the process, end-results of the process of responding. Efforts to track the process of responding *as it occurs* are rare and when undertaken have relied on the responses of expert readers of literature or on introspective accounts of the researchers themselves.

We report here on the results of a study designed to track the process of responding *as it occurs*. Pupils in individual interviews are asked to think aloud as they read a poem several times in their efforts towards meaning. The sessions are tape-recorded. The arguments for such a procedure are presented elsewhere (Dias, 1987). For our purposes it is important to say that the transcripts of these sessions – **Responding-Aloud-Protocols (RAPs)** – provide comprehensive data on the processes involved in reading poetry and the differences among readers in that respect.

The readers come to the RAP sessions after they have participated in at least ten days of small-group discussion of poetry in the non-directive procedure discussed above. Thus there is some reason to believe that they will speak from a confidence in their own responses when they are asked to say what they are thinking. The interviewer's role is to encourage the pupils to say what they are thinking and, as non-directively as possible, provide when requested the meanings of unfamiliar words. The sessions are limited to half an hour and the transcripts, averaging roughly seven pages of double-spaced type-written text, represent between 15 and 25 minutes of pupil talk. The *responding-aloud protocols* or *RAPs*, two for each of 28 pupils involved in the study, confirm that the invitation to think aloud while reading a poem is easily taken up. The responses examined were obtained from 14- and 15-year-old pupils in the middle-ability range in two mid-sized comprehensive schools in Quebec and England.

What the RAPs tell us

Analysis of the protocols reveals four patterns of reading: (1) *paraphrasing*, (2) *thematizing*, (3) *allegorizing* and (4) *problem-solving*. The reading of these four patterns is further supported by complementary data from the study. Both protocols from each pupil reveal the same pattern of reading, a pattern that is largely undeflected by differences in form and content between the two poems. The patterns will be described briefly under five headings: What the reader brings to the text, the reader's moves, closure, the reader's relationship with the text, and other elements.

I. PARAPHRASING

What the reader brings to the text
The term 'paraphrase' is used in the simple dictionary sense of restating the text in one's own words. All readers paraphrase to some extent, but *paraphrasers* adopt a stance whereby they see rendering the text in their own words as their sole responsibility. That paraphrasers see no need to push, other than in a cursory way, beyond the literal meaning of the poem suggests a rather limited conception of what the reading of poetry is about.

The reader's moves
The paraphraser has usually formed a general notion of the topic of the poem from the initial reading, a topic general enough to allow the incorporation of most details from the text. At the same time, when paraphrasers encounter elements in the text that cannot be accommodated within such an initial conception, they begin to doubt their ability to make sense of the poem; they are not, however, prepared to revise their notion of the topic to account for these elements.

After the first detailed retelling, usually following the second reading of the text, each subsequent reading is merely a consolidation and a briefer account of what was said earlier. Even when aware of gaps in their account of the poem, paraphrasers seem generally satisfied with their retellings.

Closure
Many paraphrasers seem anxious to close soon after their first or second retelling of the poem, believing that they have done what they set out to do. 'That's about it', one of them says quite often in the latter half of her protocol. Some paraphrasers feel the need to close with a moral or a lesson, a thematic statement of some kind, but such a statement is just tagged on; the poem is not re-examined in terms of this idea.

Relationship with text
Paraphrasers deal with text serially, retelling as they go along, and either

filling out the initial frame they have set for the poem, or, if the poem has a narrative structure, relating events in a temporal or causal sequence. Non-narrative text requires a great deal more inferencing on the part of the reader, guided by an initial impression or frame, and often that initial impression or frame inadequately accounts for what is sequentially revealed by the text. Paraphrasers, however, do not feel bound to account for all aspects of the text; inevitably, there are gaps in their reading.

Other features
The approach to text is serial and analytic, proceeding from an initial impression or frame. If there is synthesis, it involves merely tacking on a theme rather than drawing it out. In terms of the goals they set for themselves, paraphrasers are successful readers; the pity is their goals are so limited. For this reason primarily, they are reluctant readers of poetry.

Not all users of paraphrase stop at this point. Some readers do not see a paraphrase of the poem as the sole object of their reading but use it as a way of establishing the context and considering the possibilities of meaning. These belong to another category of readers. There are other readers who paraphrase to a considerable extent; however, because they adopt any particular interpretive frame only tentatively, they are prepared to shift their ground and reconsider the context they are working with when they encounter parts of the text that just do not fit in.

2. THEMATIZING

What the reader brings to the text
Thematizers are those readers in the study who see their task as one of finding a theme for the poem. The theme is conceived as a statement usually in the form of large generalizations about such themes as Life, Nature, Man, Animals, Landscapes or Loneliness. What especially characterizes thematizers is a notion that underlying the complexity of a poem is a rather simple theme; that, in other words, the poem is a rather complex way of saying something simple, and the reader's task is one of cracking the code. For this reason especially, the thematizer appears to be taking stabs at meaning in the expectation that somehow the theme will be tapped.

The reader's moves
Thematizers' protocols are usually disjointed. Thematizers do not appear to be working from an initial impression or controlling frame. Neither is there an attempt to paraphrase as a means of establishing the plain sense of the text. In fact, thematizers' protocols read like a series of probes for meaning, each one seemingly unrelated to the other and punctuated by long pauses.

When invited to report what he or she is thinking during these pauses, the thematizer is most likely to respond that nothing is happening during these pauses, that is, nothing that can be verbalized. What appears to be happening is that the thematizer, sensing a significance and unable to formulate it, is glancing through the text in the hope of finding something 'meaningful' to say. Working mostly at the local level, thematizers do not appear to have an overall sense of the poem against which they can test out their hypotheses. There is no cumulative build-up of meaning as one locally-developed hypothesis is set aside in order to develop another hypothesis to interpret another segment of the poem.

Closure
A closing note is sounded in the form of 'Nothing else comes to me' or 'That's all I get now.' There is a strong impression that the reader and the text have not connected, that a coherent account has not emerged. The poem has revealed several possible meanings but none that is satisfactory to the reader in accounting for the various local meanings that have come up.

Relationship with text
Thematizers work actively with the text, searching for meaning; however, while the text is attended to for meaning, it is set aside as soon as a theme is discovered.

Other features
The approach is generally analytic. Meaning is to be discovered as one searches through the text. In terms of the objectives they set for themselves, thematizers are unsuccessful readers.

3. ALLEGORIZING

Allegorizers are readers who approach a poem as though it embodies, symbolically, events or beliefs in real life. In other words, allegorizers see their task as having to work out the equivalences between the poem and life.

What the reader brings to the text
Unlike thematizers, allegorizers look at the poem as a whole and read the poem guided by an overall impression or frame. They are similar to paraphrasers in that respect, except that they conceive their task as more than merely reporting the plain sense of the poem. Instead they work on formulating a statement about life as it is presented by and can be construed from the poem. Often such statements represent stock notions carried from past experience, particularly with literature. Allegorizers approach the poem with a strong expectation that the poem will make sense. We expect this is so because they seem so much more to direct the process by a controlling idea than other readers do; that is, they assume the responsibility for making sense.

The reader's moves
Most allegorizers work from a strong feeling or intuition about the poem. 'I get this feeling of loneliness', says one. Their basic move is to formulate a broad generalization about life or nature and develop that generalization to accord with the details of the poem. The process is one of aligning aspects of the text with the aspects of the meaning that is being developed: 'this' in the text means 'that' in life. Textual details that do not accord with this meaning are set aside or realigned to fit. Those initial impressions prove to be powerful in directing the reading of the poem. They appear to develop from an open stance to the poem's meaning and are hard to shake, once they appear to accord with the poem's basic details. 'I keep getting that', says one reader referring to a persisting early impression, and later, 'That's what I get.' No two ways about it.

Closure
Allegorizers tend to be satisfied with their efforts in making sense of the poem. They are aware of gaps in their interpretations but do not believe that these are indicative of flaws in their basic interpretations.

Reader's relationship to text
Allegorizers tend to twist the text to fit the meaning they are creating but some are less oblivious than others to the demands they are making on the text, saying they are not sure of this and that aspect of their interpretation. At the same time, they are not willing to develop and consider a hypothesis that might better accommodate the inconsistencies they sense.

Other elements
The allegorizer's approach to text is basically synthetic. Allegorizers draw on those aspects of the text that support their meaning and ignore those that do not. They are analytic to the extent that they are able to sort out and fit those aspects to their meaning.

4. PROBLEM-SOLVING

What the reader brings to the text
Problem-solvers are a group of readers whose approach to making sense of poetry is to try a variety of strategies towards that end. More than the readers in the other categories, they approach the poem with enthusiasm for the task ahead. They are alert to possibilities of meaning and to connections between the poem and their own experience.

The reader's moves
Problem-solvers do not all operate in the same way. If they share a common trait, it is a refusal to settle immediately on meaning and, rather, to be

tentative in their formulations of meaning. It is not that they do not trust themselves as readers; rather, they see poetry as a complex artifact that does not easily reveal its meaning. Thus they are tolerant of ambiguity and willing to postpone dealing with apparent blocks to understanding until they have taken another run through the poem in the hope of achieving a perspective that might disentangle the difficulties and eliminate the ambiguity. But they are not easily satisfied; and time and time again, they announce their puzzlement and return to problematical areas. Problem-solvers also share a common approach in that they use a variety of strategies to make sense of poetry. The chief and most successful strategy is setting and testing several hypotheses in the effort towards meaning. The hypotheses are not merely pulled out of thin air. Problem-solvers probe their own experience for analogous clues and search actively through the text for cues that might point to what is happening.

There are other strategies as well. Problem-solvers distinguish themselves from other kinds of readers in the variety of means they employ in working towards an understanding of poetry. Thus like other readers they turn as much to feelings and intuitions to direct their reading. They also use paraphrasing, not as the major strategy but as one more means of enhancing their understanding. More than readers in the other categories, problem-solvers tend to visualize what is happening in the poem: they get 'flashes' and images and pictures.

Closure
Problem-solvers generally tend to delay closure. Like readers in other categories as well, they sense there is something in the poem they 'just haven't got' or 'can't get'; but unlike these other readers, problem-solvers consider it their responsibility to find out. Such delay of closure is also likely to derive from their having experienced poetry as a continuing unfolding of meaning. For them, a poem is never ever fully understood.

Relationship with text
More than among the other kinds of readers, there is an active interplay between the text and the reader. Problem-solvers do not abandon the text once they feel they have a workable hypothesis; neither do they dwell at the level of text without one or more tentative hypotheses in mind. Because of this respect for the integrity of the text, problem-solvers almost always catch their own misreadings or miscues.

Other elements
The problem-solver's approach to the text is primarily synthetic. The effort after meaning is directed by an overall awareness of several possibilities of meaning and a gradual narrowing down of those possibilities. The stance is

tentative. Of all readers interviewed, problem-solvers appear to be most aware of their own processes in reading poetry.

Discussion

Several points need to be made, however briefly:

1 Even though these patterns are easily and consistently ascribable to particular individuals in the group and reappear in protocols obtained from these individuals a year later, one needs to remember that these are *patterns of reading* rather than patterns of readers.
2 These patterns describe initial encounters with a poem only, a part of the process of responding. Yet in the eyes of many teachers who have read the RAPs, the process recorded there goes a lot further than they are used to seeing in their own teacher-directed classrooms.
3 Set against the actual protocols, these accounts seem rather flat, mere abstractions of what actually occurs during reading. It is in the RAPs, four of which are presented in Chapter 4, that one senses the reader's movements of thought, particularly when these protocols are read besides the poems they derive from. These accounts also create the impression that the poems are read but not felt or experienced. Unfortunately, the RAPs do not record directly the experiential aspects of response, except where these are explicitly stated. Clearly, several readers were guided by impressions, feelings and images, by what they sensed rather than only by what they had deciphered.
4 There are clear differences in the protocols among the pupils who allow themselves, as Dixon once put it, 'the luxury of being wrong' and those who do not. One can ascribe key aspects of some patterns to the school practices that likely engendered them. On the other hand, there is reason to believe that some pupils' problem-solving patterns could not be attributed to what had gone on in their literature classes.
5 The patterns are obviously interrelated. Paraphrasers and allegorizers proceed serially, while thematizers and problem-solvers are to a large extent holists. One might think of paraphrasers and allegorizers as surveyors who map the terrain – the paraphraser with little sense of what lies beneath the surface and the allegorizer who can read the topography and give a fairly general picture of underground formations. The thematizer is a miner who acts on hunches to dig in various places in the hope of finding a rich vein. The problem-solver is both surveyor and miner; he scans and he probes; he is not anxious to close; he knows there is more.

The usefulness of this study lies in its alerting teachers to the differences among readers in their ways of making sense of poetry and the extent to which classroom practices contribute to the expectations that help shape these patterns. Chapter 4 provides with commentary the texts of four RAPs, not merely to illustrate how these patterns are represented in actual readings, but to enable readers to sense the rich variety and range of abilities these protocols represent. Knowing what goes on and can go on as readers meet a poem, we might wish to consider how we can create the kinds of classroom communities that take account of such richness and variety.

4 Four readers reading

We believe that the convincingness of the theory and research drawn on in earlier chapters lies largely in the convergences they represent: reading poetry is a complex activity; the contexts of reading, readers' expectations and stances, for instance, determine powerfully the nature of the literary transaction; poems do not 'mean' in and of themselves and are not as fixed and stable in the meanings they purvey as they have often been regarded. We also believe that these principles and findings will draw conviction from the everyday experiences of teachers and readers of poetry. This chapter presents the transcripts of actual readings of a poem. We expect these Responding–Aloud–Protocols (RAPs) to give substance to our argument and provide evidence of the genuine abilities of adolescent readers. When people ask what happens in the transaction between reader and poem and how readers differ in the ways they go about making sense of poetry, we would like to point in answer to the four readings below.

The readings are the texts with explanatory commentary of four RAPs in response to Ted Hughes' 'The Thought-Fox'. These particular RAPs have been selected because they are fairly representative of the four patterns of reading described in Chapter 3. The 16-year-old readers are in the fifth-form of a comprehensive school in Cambridgeshire, England and, based on school assessments and teachers' judgements, are in the middle-ability range. Readers should remember that the RAPs represent initial stages in the transaction between reader and poem; they do not record what occurs in later re-readings as the poem settles into a larger network of thoughts, feelings and experiences, including experiences of other literary and non-literary texts. At the same time, such initial encounters provide clues to how meanings develop and are established, as well as information on the attitudes and expectations that to a large extent direct how the poem will continue to be read.

The poem

The Thought-Fox

I imagine this midnight moment's forest:
Something else is alive
Beside the clock's loneliness
And this blank page where my fingers move.

Through the window I see no star: 5
Something more near
Though deeper within darkness
Is entering the loneliness:

Cold, delicately as the dark snow,
A fox's nose touches twig, leaf;   10
Two eyes serve a movement, that now
And again now, and now, and now

Sets neat prints into the snow
Between trees, and warily a lame
Shadow lags by stump and in hollow   15
Of a body that is bold to come

Across clearings, an eye,
A widening deepening greenness,
Brilliantly, concentratedly,
Coming about its own business   20

Till, with a sudden sharp hot stink of fox
It enters the dark hole of the head.
The window is starless still; the clock ticks,
The page is printed.

                                                          Ted Hughes

Perhaps it is best to begin by reading what Ted Hughes has to say about
this poem:

> This poem does not have anything you could easily call a meaning. It is about
> a fox, obviously enough, but a fox is both a fox and not a fox. What sort of fox
> is it that can step right into my head where presumably it still sits . . . smiling
> to itself when the dogs bark. It is both a fox and a spirit. It is a real fox; as I
> read the poem I see it move, I see it setting its prints, I see its shadow going
> over the irregular surface of the snow. The words show me all this, bringing it
> nearer and nearer . . .
>   . . . As it is, every time I read the poem the fox comes up again out of the
> darkness and steps into my head (1969, p. 20).

Perhaps the poem is also about the creative imagination and its metaphorical
foxiness – the fox that is thought and the thought that is a fox. Perhaps, as we
might learn from these four readers, there are possibilities of meaning that

have not entered *our* heads. Before reading the RAPs, it might help to re-read the poem to have a surer sense of one's own response and then consider what aspects of the poem are likely to appeal, what signs of key recognitions one should look for in the RAPs, and where, if any, are the likely stumbling blocks.

The readings

Most of the text of the RAPs is reproduced below. Parts of the text have been summarized where this could be done without misrepresenting the substance of the response. The thinking–aloud is not as continuous as it may appear below. The actual RAP transcripts are punctuated by several conversational responses intended to encourage the flow of talk. The interviewer's comments are reproduced only where they represent a substantial contribution to the conversation. Pauses in the RAPs are indicated by three dots (. . .). They represent normal hesitations of up to about five seconds. Longer pauses are indicated either as (. . . pause), (long pause), or, when over a minute, by the actual length of the pause. Parts of the RAP that could not be made out are indicated by (??). 'False starts' and fillers (such as 'hmmm') have been retained only where they might help inform our understanding of the reader's progress through the poem.

Peter

Peter is 16 years old, of average ability, and plans to enlist in the armed forces. He says he does not particularly like to read poetry. He is not an avid reader, though he prefers adventure novels when he does choose to read.

After the interviewer has read the poem, Peter is asked if he has any initial reactions. After some hesitation, he responds:

> . . . it's about a fox – that's what it is who (??) . . . and then he says: 'through the window I see no star'; perhaps it's somebody – you know like it's a . . . forest and he can see quite a bit and he's just or he's imagining what's in the forest.

Peter's first reaction is to say what the poem is about and what is happening. He confirms that this is only his first impression and asks if he should read the poem. He reads the poem aloud and after an encouraging nod from the interviewer:

> I think the last line and somewhere . . . further up – the fourth line it talks about a page – so perhaps it's somebody who is reading a book and just imagining . . . that they are in a forest and he can see a fox . . . and it's all its movements or something. (Long pause – sighs.)

With this second reading, Peter realizes that he must somehow find the thread that links 'page' with the fox and settles on someone 'reading a book and just imagining'. The long pause and the sigh indicate considerable uncertainty about this line of thinking. It turns out, after some hesitation: 'I'm sure the person who is talking . . . can see the fox.' He is asked to clarify:

> I think it's real – 'cause he certainly goes through it with quite a bit of . . . description for what the fox is doing. So I would think that – the person could actually see it – than he's more imagining it . . . (pause). Maybe the fox is out hunting or something, at night . . . (pause).

Peter had begun by assuming that the fox is imagined; however, the descriptive details suggest otherwise. He pauses, studies the poem, and is asked what he's looking at. He goes on hesitatingly:

> I'm just looking at this last one. . . . 'cause it looks – trying to work out the a – the first two lines is about a fox – what he's doing and the last two he's . . . it's as though the person is inside . . . a house . . . looking at the fox or looking at the forest or something. . . . I don't see what that – 'the clock ticks' means – about someone who's got the fox? The clock – 'beside the clock's loneliness'. . . . Or maybe a . . . that the person who is talking is . . . a bit quite lonely as well and he's perhaps . . . comparing himself with the clock you know he's got – the clock's got nothing to do either I suppose.

Peter is concerned to establish the details of the setting and the place of the speaker and the fox in this setting. He wonders whether the ticking clock is intended to accentuate the speaker's loneliness.

> (Pause) But it still goes on about 'the page is . . .' Maybe the person is just reading a book – about the fox . . . and . . . probably now and then he gets sort of distracted and looks out the window – and begins imagining it. . . . What is happening in the book could be happening just outside his house or something.

Peter still holds on to the frame that someone is reading a book: the book is about a fox, a fox who could be imagined lurking outside the house as well. After a long pause, the interviewer asks whether Peter might wish to think aloud a stanza at a time.

> Yeah I could do it (long pause as he reads). Oh first two [lines] it says 'I imagine this midnight moment's forest' – so maybe the person is imagining it and can't actually see anything. He's imagining something else is alive, you know, a fox; and he's . . . just sitting back imagining things like. . . . Maybe he's quite lonely and he's comparing himself to the clock in the third line. . . . And he's reading a book I suppose . . .

Thus far Peter is merely consolidating what he has said. He goes on:

> The poet talks about the page . . . and as he . . . 'and this blank page where my fingers move'. Maybe he's sort of turning the page over, and as he's doing that he just sort of has a little rest from reading and looks out the window, and

imagines or something. . . . And he says, 'Through the window I see no star'
– so maybe he's looking out the window then . . . (pause). I don't know what
those three lines [points to: 'Something more near / Though deeper within
darkness / Is entering the loneliness:'], what they're supposed to mean. . . .
What do I do about this?

The interviewer suggests after a long pause that Peter put those lines aside
and come back to them later. The scenario that Peter has built up of a
speaker reading about a fox and imagining it outside the house as well
cannot easily accommodate those three lines.

Okay . . . (pause). The next two lines, perhaps . . . what is happening in the
book – the person is reading and perhaps it's quite cold and snowing outside
as well, so he sort of . . . thinks back to what was written in the book and he
imagines a fox just outside, sniffing around or hunting. . . . And the 'two eyes
serve a movement' perhaps a . . . the fox is very tense and you know sort of
looking about all the time, I think, making sure nothing is coming or looking
at him. . . . I think 'sets neat prints into the snow' . . . it's a, that means he's
walking very carefully . . . because if he was running all the snow would sort
of get messed up if he's . . . kind of very carefully puts his foot down cleanly
between all the trees, you know, it's sort of hiding . . . (pause). Kind of
like . . . and maybe something following him . . . a shadow . . . I'm not
really sure about that.

What the RAPs make clear are the several possibilities of meaning that are
open to readers. 'A lame shadow' need not be the fox's own shadow, and
thus invites the notion that the fox is quite likely being followed. By a
hunter, perhaps? As in another part of the RAP above, Peter acknowledges
those parts of the text he is uncertain about. Some readers tend not to
recognize aspects of the poem they cannot accommodate within the meaning
they are constructing.

(Pause) I think this next bit, the fox is perhaps coming to an opening in the
wood . . . and . . . maybe it's getting towards the morning . . . he says, 'a
widening deepening greenness', so perhaps, you know, the sun is beginning
to come up and he can see all the green, you know, the grass and that, so . . .
(pause). Yeah, he's sort of – I think that's probably right because like when it
says . . . because the . . . it enters down the – it goes down a dark hole and I
suppose his . . . den . . . you know, going home for the day or something –
until next . . . night.

It is interesting how 'widening' and 'greenness' are associated not with the
'eye' but with sunrise. And in support of such an interpretation, Peter offers
the contrasting darkness of the fox's den and the fox's return to sleep out the
day. By the way, quite a few readers interpret 'dark hole' as the fox's den.
Having done so, they retain the hole–den connection firmly in their minds
and are unlikely to relinquish that frame even when they realize later that

the speaker is writing and the fox is imagined in the act of that writing. Peter goes on:

> Uhmm . . . that bit about right at the beginning – I've just seen that line . . . it says a 'and this blank page where my fingers move' . . . perhaps it's a writer . . . who's trying to think of . . . he's writing a book or something and he's written so much but he's just trying to think of something to write about a fox in a story. And he's imagined all of the poem, and then the last line it says the page is printed; so maybe he's written it, all that, in his book.

The interviewer asks how Peter had come to this interpretation.

> I don't know; I just came down to the bottom and it says the page is printed, and I suddenly thought back to the blank page . . .

That he had not noticed the conjunction of these particular lines is not surprising. Working on some kind of best-fit strategy, readers often ignore information that they are unable to accommodate within the hypothesis they are building. Their experience with poetry is likely that not everything in a poem makes sense immediately and will likely fall into place as their understanding grows or when the teacher 'explains' the poem.

> And, you know, looking out the window trying to get a few more ideas and that sort of thing. . . . Perhaps this clock ticks business is a. . . . Maybe because it's very quiet in his room, you know, . . . he's just thinking so; maybe the clock ticking . . . makes quite a noise really, so . . . (pause) (sighs) . . .

The interviewer reminds Peter to say what he is thinking.

> I was just trying to – I was just going through the whole thing and trying to see if I could see anything else. . . . (pause) . . . (sighs) . . . No, I can't see anything else there – I sort of know what those three lines are . . .

The interviewer finds out Peter is referring to 'Something more near / Though deeper within darkness / Is entering the loneliness', the very lines he had put aside earlier as problematical. They still remain problematical; so the interviewer offers to read the poem once through again. Following the reading:

> Perhaps this, near line 15, it's perhaps about what the fox has caught – it's 'Between trees, and warily a lame / Shadow' – it's perhaps, I don't know, the fox is dragging it or something . . . 'lags by stump' – so I don't know; perhaps he's . . . bitten his tail off and he's got a little stump and he's got . . . he's pulling it along by that . . . or perhaps it could be, you know, as I said someone . . . something following him – I don't know . . . (pause).

In an attempt to accommodate 'shadow', 'drags' and 'stump', Peter creates a scenario that contradicts what he had said earlier about the fox being followed. When the interviewer asks how this reading has helped his understanding of the poem, whether it all falls into place, Peter responds: 'More than when I first read it.' The interviewer asks Peter how he perceives the poem after these several readings: 'What's happening in your mind?'

> Somebody . . . looking out of a window . . . imagining I think . . . – no, it's not happening in real life – the person is just imagining it . . . (pause). I don't see anything else though.

He is asked what is being imagined.

> What is happening, what the fox is doing – you know in . . . during the night wandering around, perhaps hunting . . . just being nosey . . . (pause).

He is reminded to say what he is thinking.

> I'll just go through it again and see if I could see anything else, but I don't think I can; but I still don't know what those three lines mean.

He is again referring to the same three lines (6–9), and is asked if he thinks they are important to his understanding of the poem. He answers that he does not think so. He is asked about the last stanza.

> I think that means the fox is going home – in this dark hole . . . and a . . . this writer person . . . he's perhaps . . . can't sort of think of anything else to write about the fox; so he sort of just says, you know, that the fox goes home. His window is still starless, so perhaps he's still looking out of the window. . . . And then a . . . he goes down to write what he's imagined . . . And the page is printed.

Interestingly, little has changed in Peter's account of the poem except that certain 'facts' have become more established. He is asked how he feels about the poem as a poem and responds that he quite likes it. Pressed to say what he likes about it, he specifies, 'the fox's movements and that sort of thing'.

Peter seems to have perceived his task of reading as one largely of saying what happened in the poem, of providing an account that accommodates as much of the information as is provided by the poem within a consistent framework. This account is not easily arrived at, and he knows that there are certain lines he has not accommodated within the meaning he has constructed; however, it is unlikely that he considers his reading as inadequate or a failure. In terms of the patterns of reading described in the previous chapter, Peter's reading is very much within the pattern described as paraphrasing.

Martin

Martin is 16 years old and says he is fond of reading. His school performance, according to school records and teacher assessments, is slightly below average. He is friendly and outgoing, eager to talk. Immediately after the interviewer has read the poem, he says:

I think that there is a boy inside his bedroom (this is my impression) and he is looking out his window and . . . I think he's got up in the middle of the night, after maybe – well, maybe he has read a book . . . something about maybe frost or something, then he looks out the window and then imagines seeing – no, not imagining but I think he could (??) fox's 'cause it said – I'm not sure where was it. . . . I think it could be as it snowed. It says here it snowed – the moon's out, think the moon is bright and it reflects off as nicely you can see everything.

Martin is untypical of most readers for the confidence with which he offers this initial account. He seems to dart about over the poem picking up bits here and there. Thus he goes on to say that the bright moonlight (which he may have inferred from 'brilliantly') allows the 'boy' to see everything, including the fox making footprints in the snow. In order to say so, he must ignore 'darkness' and 'no star'. He continues to elaborate on his initial response:

So he's looking what the fox is doing 'cause it says here: 'A fox's nose touches twig, leaf.' I think that it sort of – the fox is very wary where it's going, but I think it's never been at this place before, so it's sort of smelling out, you know. 'Two eyes serve a moment [the interviewer says, 'movement']' yeah, movement, . . . I'm not too sure about, maybe the fox (in that paragraph I think it's talking about the fox); he's standing still, you know, not moving at all but just moving his eyes – you know he's looking around and you know as it says here: 'And again now, and now, and now' – I think he's saying to himself, 'Well, there he moves again and again and again.' The boy is looking out the window and he . . . is very interested in what the fox is doing. I think that's what that means here, so it's quite feasible. . . . (pause).

He is reminded to say what he is thinking.

I'm just trying to read it through and thinking of ideas. . . . (pause). He or she is imagining this midnight moment's forest. So he could be having a dream. . . . 'Something else is alive / Beside the clock's loneliness.' Yeah I think he is definitely reading a book.

The first line now suggests a dream to him, but he quickly reverts to saying the boy is reading a book. Asked why he believes so, he cites 'this blank page', but again almost immediately changes his mind:

No, no. I think whatever that means, he is looking out the window and he – and the blank page he thinks is snow. Of course, yeah?

But he returns to the dream hypothesis again:

So he could be dreaming; he could be thinking in his mind that there is nothing there. So I mean just he is *not* looking out the window or anything, he just could be lying down on his bed and his mind is completely blank, 'cause he's sleeping and he's tired out, and I must fit it down here.

That last remark is revealing. Martin tends to flesh out his hypotheses with little regard to what is offered in the poem. Having suggested the 'lying on bed' hypothesis and its expansion, he checks to see how it fits in with the text.

> He's down on his bed, you know, and he thinks that – his mind is not thinking of anything but he, he can see, he can feel something moving in his mind or something thinking in his mind. Ahh that's not, that's not a very good idea . . . (pause).

Interestingly, he senses the movement of the fox in the speaker's mind, but does not recognize how central that notion is.

> For some reason it doesn't sort of work; I prefer the idea when he is looking out the window. I'd like to go along with that one; but I'm sure there is another idea. I am just trying to think. There is completely quiet, so I think that could imply that it is dark. Everybody is asleep, you know, because it says 'beside the clock's loneliness'. Do you think that could mean the clock's on the mantlepiece and next to it there could be a picture of snow and he is looking at it? There could be a fox, made some imprints in the snow, and he's pricked his ears. He is looking at one thing; might be he's put his nose down into the (??) [snow].

Quite clearly Martin works at the local level, developing hypotheses from a phrase or a sentence, and then developing details to apply to the poem and realizing quickly 'it doesn't sort of work'. We may recall above: 'I'm just trying to read it through and looking for ideas.' The interviewer asks if he is speaking of the fox as present in the picture of snow.

> Yeah, that's in the picture. . . . Or it could be that the clock could be next to a window. . . . And he is sitting down on the chair looking out of a window. You can see the fox moving making imprints in the snow. It could be that. Do you know what I mean?
>
> He's looking out through the window and he can see these things. [Glances at the text] That's interesting: 'Through the window I see no star'; apparently that's the hard. . . . Those two it's really hard. 'Something more near / Though deep within darkness / it enters [is entering] the loneliness.' I think that could be the fox moving into something; he's moving further into loneliness, if you like. He's moving further out from his window and he's moving out into the forest maybe, you know into deeper darkness than it, than it is outside.
>
> It's hard to make sense of this verse . . . it's hard to read in between the lines; because it doesn't make sense if you don't, you know.

For Martin, it seems reading poetry is a matter of reading between the lines; puzzling out the poem; making good guesses. He continues to puzzle over the second stanza:

> 'Through the window I see no star:' . . . 'Through the window I see no star:' . . . I'm blank about that . . . (pause). It might not be a fox at all!

He pauses and the interviewer reminds him to say what he is thinking.

> Just trying to think of another solution. It might not be a fox at all; he could be referring to something else . . . 'Two eyes serve a movement', it could mean that it is a picture, . . . someone could be taking a picture of this – the fox, you know, and his movement catches, no his eye catches the particular moment.

The interviewer asks whose eye he is referring to.

> The cameras' [camera's?] eyes and . . . that's not a very good idea now either. This is a hard poem. . . . That [Two eyes serve a movement] is quite a hard line. It could be a human, it could be an animal, it could be . . . I'm not sure.

He tries to set the line in context.

> And again now, and now, and now, two eyes serve a movement . . . so it must be very still outside, no wind. Nothing at all, just the fox moving. So looking through the window, two eyes serve a movement – I think I've got it here, hold it: he's looking through the window and all that is moving is the fox, nothing else. . . . And the fox only moves very rarely because, as I said before, it could be it was not his own territory. He's looking around for some other – predatory you know – so I think that could be it. It might not be a boy at all in his house; it could be something else.

Once more he makes a new hypothesis, derived primarily from the struggle with a particular line, but displacing earlier hypotheses. When asked what has made him change his mind, he responds:

> You see I'm not sure; I'm trying to find different clues to the answer, and I'm asking myself all these different questions, 'cause I might come up with something, you see. It might not even be a boy, . . . [reads first line]. It could be a painter coming up with a solution to . . . nah, nah.

For the next few minutes Martin advances several hypotheses deriving from 'something else is alive' and all centring round the notion that the painter wishes to add movement to the stillness. Having looked at the first three verses, he decides to look at the others. He focuses on 'Of a body that is bold to come,' and decides it has something to do with the fox's looking for his food:

> It could mean that soon . . . he could have his food. 'Shadow lags by stump and in hollow' [repeated three times]: that's a hard one . . . God, that is a hard line. 'Sets neat prints into the snow' – so I think the fox is moving. . . . It could have moved and stopped and then looking for its prey. 'Between trees . . . a lame shadow lags by stump' – the fox could be going off to something – maybe the fox has got it already, his prey. . . . Because it's lame, isn't it? Maybe his leg or something is injured. It's moving [not smoothly]. The fox is following his prey, . . . he's smelling the twigs and that for its scent . . . between trees . . . hollow – it could be a rabbit, couldn't it? . . .
> . . . 'Across clearings, an eye' – that's another hard verse – 'A widening

deepening greenness, / Across clearings, an eye' – I think that means that . . . the snow is melting . . . yeah I think that the snow is . . . Oh I find that verse . . . I know what that means. He's saying that the snow is slightly melting away. . . . 'Brilliantly, concentratedly, / Coming about its own business /' – It's doing it by its own business . . . at what speed it likes, when it likes. . . .

And in the end the fox has got his prey. I think that's what it could be saying in the last verse: 'Till, with a sudden sharp hot stink of fox it / [reads the last verse].

. . . I think I've got the last verse. . . . He's woken up in the middle of the night – there's just the moon out and it's snowing . . . it says here in the fifth verse that the snow is melting; so it's coming to the end of winter. . . . He's looked through his window and he's trying to sum up . . . that night and he's put it down into a poem. I think that's what he's done.

The syntax of the poem can present problems for some readers; however, as we shall see with some other readers, it does not defeat reading for what is basically going on. Martin's notion of the melting snow ('deepening greenness') is at the expense of ignoring 'eye'. The shadow becomes the fox's prey, and a moonlit night prevails over the darkness. But there are several clues as to how Martin's concerted efforts after meaning take him to where he is. Martin is asked how he arrived at the meaning he now has settled on:

I sort of, summed up each verse and I think I've come to the decision that in the end the fox has got his prey . . . 'cause he went down a hole and that's it. You know that's what happens and he runs off; that's the end of the story, if you like, 'cause it says the page is printed.

. . . The window is starless still, so when you look through the window there is nothing to move, . . . and also 'the page is printed' means the fox has come along, printed all its feet in the snow and he's gone off and done his bit, you know, for the night. . . . I think that's what it means.

Martin is reminded that he had said something about a poem being written.

Yeah, I think the poet just looked through his window one night and he saw all this happening, and he started putting it down maybe in his diary or whatever; I think he put it down in a poem.

In the effort towards meaning, Martin has generated several hypotheses. It has been a trial and error method mainly, deriving not from an overall sense of what is happening but rather from whatever is suggested by particular lines and verses. Much of the RAP, for instance, is taken up by his dwelling on the first three verses. Martin's pattern of reading fits well within what we have called the thematizing pattern. He reads the poem as though it were a puzzle; it is a concerted effort at searching for meaning, but the search is piecemeal and haphazard.

Carol

Carol is 16 years old, not very talkative, reads regularly, a book about every two weeks (mostly fiction) and plans to attend university. She is regarded by her teachers as being above average in ability.

The interviewer reads the poem and asks for her first impressions. Carol says, 'I don't know', and asks if she can read the poem herself. She reads the poem silently, pauses for a while and when prodded to say what she is thinking, responds:

> I don't know . . . (pause). I don't understand. 'I imagine this midnight moment's forest . . .' (pause).

What Carol hopes to have realized in her initial readings is some sense of what is going on in this poem. When asked what she has realized thus far, she shows she is having difficulty finding her bearings in the poem:

> Is it someone sitting inside? I don't know . . . and then, when they look out the window . . . 'cold, delicately as the dark snow' . . . I'm not sure if this is what's happening but – they see a fox or the person sees a fox . . . (pause) . . . Hmmm (laughs) . . . He is minding his own business but then . . . I don't know . . . till 'a sudden sharp hot stink of fox / It enters the dark hole of the head' . . . well, just by reading the lines, something happens to the fox and the person is left as he began.

Unlike some other readers, Carol wishes to establish first a frame within which she can read the poem. She proceeds quite tentatively; in only 12 lines of transcript she has repeated 'I don't know', or a similar phrase at least six times. Thus far she can say with some certainty only that something happens to the fox and the person is left unchanged. She decides to read the poem and comment as she goes along.

> 'And this blank page where my fingers move' . . . so he's written a page . . . starless and the clock ticks . . . (long pause).

Clearly, Carol is not reading the text in a linear sequence; her eye has taken lines 4 and 24 in one glance. She is obviously trying to work out a pattern of relationships. She is reminded to say what she is thinking.

> I'm trying to see . . . what's happened to the clock – the clock ticks, it's lonely, . . . (sighs) . . . and it's still a starless night . . . I don't [know] what the fox . . . what the thought-fox . . . (mumbles) . . . 'something else is alive' . . . (pause).

She is asked to say what she is thinking.

> I don't know, I don't know what this . . . (mumbles) . . . a star, something near . . . (pause) . . . I don't know. . . . What is the fox a symbol of or anything? Does it, does it, . . . sly? Is that it?

The interviewer responds that some people think the fox is sly. Carol asks if that means anything and is told it is up to her to decide. She replies (for the eleventh time), 'I don't know.' From two earlier RAPs, it is clear that Carol's readings are directed very much by an initial strong impression of what the poem is about, what one might call an intuited, felt sense. This time, she is less possessed by this felt sense. All she has to guide her is an impression that 'something happens to the fox and the person is left as he began'. Pressed to continue, she takes another run through the poem:

> 'I imagine this midnight moment's forest' . . . (pause). . . . Okay there is some . . . 'And this blank page where my fingers move' . . . (long pause).

She is urged to say what she is thinking.

> Okay, okay, he is imagining this midnight moment's forest; he is imagining a forest with a fox in it. 'Something else is alive' . . . 'Cause he is writing; he is a writer I guess. 'Through the window I see no star, / Something more near' – Okay that's him looking out the window but not seeing what's in front of him – He's looking – 'Something more near / Though deeper within darkness / Is entering the loneliness:' . . . He [the writer] is trying to get into his imagination I think. . . .
>   'Cold, delicately as the dark snow'. . . . Okay and he starts imagining a fox . . . (mumbles) . . . 'That now / And again now, and now', I don't know.

She backs up to the previous line to garner more of the context:

> 'Two eyes serve, serve a moment, movement . . . Two eyes serve a movement that now' – I don't know what 'now and again now, now, now' means.

Carol is reading basically to establish the plain sense of the poem, a procedure that was often used during the group work in the early stages of a discussion. Some of the problems that are quite typically faced in reading poetry are apparent here, particularly because many readers often read as though each line is an independent unit of meaning. Carol has backed up a line and not managed to make sense; the interviewer suggests that she read on to the next line as well.

> Okay, that's just him moving on . . . the fox . . . 'warily a lame / Shadow lags by stump' . . . (pause) . . . I find it gives the impression that he's wounded – I guess – 'and in hollow / . . . Of a body that is bold to come . . . bold to come . . . Across clearings . . . an eye, a widening deepening greenness', . . . Okay he [the author] has this imagination switch . . .
>   He is looking out the window and he imagines a fox and it's dark and it's cold and it's a forest and then . . . I don't know . . . he follows the fox across clearings . . . 'an eye / A widening deepening greenness / Brilliantly, concentratedly, / Coming about its own business' . . . Oh, okay, the fox is just wandering around till 'with a sudden sharp hot stink of fox it enters the dark hole of the head – it enters' . . . (long pause).

The interviewer prods Carol to say what she thinks is happening.

> I think he [the fox] gets shot in the head . . . and the writer goes back to . . .
> not his imagination . . . 'The window is starless still' . . . [but back to] kind
> of real life for him and he's written a page. He has written what he has seen or
> what he has imagined.

This run through the poem has helped her realize an outline or shape of
what is going on in the poem. It is interesting that she is not bogged down by
local details. When she finally sorts out lines 11–13, she has no more to say
than, 'Okay, that's just him moving on.' But she does register impressions: 'I
find it gives the impression that he's wounded.'

The interviewer asks how she feels about her understanding of the poem.
Her response is telling in its directness:

> The words are clear but I am not sure what . . . the meaning is or
> something . . . (very long pause). The thought-fox . . . I don't know (sighs).

Many readers would not distinguish in the way that Carol does between
knowing what the words mean and knowing the meaning 'or something'. If
we go by her other RAPs, that something is a sense of how the events in the
poem relate to events in real life. While such a goal is not consciously
elaborated by Carol, this has really been an underlying concern in her other
readings. Looking only to establish what is going on in the poem and then
hoping to discover what lies beyond the poem, she tends not to attend
consciously to specific phrasings unless they register in an impression, a clue
to deeper or further meaning. She agrees to re-read the poem, and reads it
aloud this time.

> I think, I don't know, the person, the writer – I think there is a writer in this –
> he gets an idea. It could be at the same time as – you know when I thought the
> fox got shot in the head – it could also be the writer getting a thought in his
> head.

She offers this suggestion hesitantly ('I don't know', 'could be'). She pauses
for a while, and then:

> Oh no, . . . when I just read that last paragraph, and . . . I wasn't sure before
> about it but then I read it, and if I read it closer to the last two lines instead of
> close to the first line, then it said about the . . . a man who is blind; but if I
> read it close to the top line, then it would have . . . then the fox is getting shot
> in the head.

Interestingly, this is the first reference in the RAP to 'blindness'. As with
some of the other RAPs on this poem, fingers moving on a page, even if it is a
blank page, convey the impression of a blind reader. In Carol's case the
impression has registered and remains unexamined. What she seems to be
suggesting are alternative readings determined by which particular lines

frame her understanding. The interviewer asks which interpretation seems more sensible.

> . . . (pause) I don't know if one is more sensible than the other, because . . . It must be the fox getting shot in the head, I think, because . . . 'a sharp stink of fox', that, and its minding its own business and its just coming along, till 'with a sudden sharp hot stink of fox / It enters the dark hole of the head' – I don't know . . .

The interviewer asks what the 'it' that enters the dark hole of the head refers to. Carol believes it is the bullet; and the interviewer asks whether a bullet has been mentioned earlier in the poem.

> I don't know. What else could it be? . . . (sighs) I don't think there is anything else it could be . . . (sighs – long pause).

She is asked to re-read the poem once more in the light of all that has emerged thus far. She reads the first stanza aloud and stops to comment.

> He is going to create something else 'cause 'something else is alive / Beside the clock's loneliness / hmmm . . . and this blank page where my fingers move.' . . . (long pause) . . . Loneliness keeps on popping up.
> Hmmm . . . 'I imagine this midnight' . . . 'beside the clock's loneliness' . . . Well, if he's alone and . . . no, the clock is the only thing that's making noise . . . Until . . . (sighs) . . . until he starts seeing the fox and imagining there is a fox coming along. . . . (sighs) . . . (long pause).

Carol's sighing is not a sign of stress; it indicates rather that she is aware of discrepancies between what she senses and wishes to report and what she can point to in the poem to account for it. As she pauses for some time, the interviewer reminds her to report what she is thinking.

> I'm trying to compare the way the poem began in the beginning and how it ended. . . . (pause). There is still no stars outside, still the clock ticking away, but the page has been written. . . . So that means he's . . . (long pause) Yeah, he's created the fox, 'cause the fox, . . . 'something else is alive', he says, right? And then down here, well if I was right about it being a bullet, the fox isn't alive anymore; it's just on paper . . . (long pause). And if we didn't do what we kind of did in that one . . . (??)
> Say the image, the contrast in image – there is 'dark snow' up here, and there is 'deepening greenness' down here . . . (sighs) . . . It's becoming clearer, I think – clearer to the writer, I think . . . (pause) . . . And there's a . . . he's just thinking, it's coming out as a stream . . . Wait a minute.

The interviewer asks what is coming out as a stream.

> His ideas and what he sees – it's his own business . . . (pause) Hmmmhmmm (hums) 'Though deeper within darkness it's entering the loneliness' . . . (pause). And he is cold and everything . . . 'A fox's nose touches twig . . . sets neat prints . . .' [reads lines 10–13]. So he's just thought of the fox and

'into the snow between trees / and warily a lame shadow lags in stump and in hollow' . . . hmmm.

(whispers . . . long pause). Okay, wait, there is . . . 'Two eyes serve a movement . . . hollow' . . . [reads lines 11–14]. The fox is all tired I guess – or is it? . . . 'neat prints' can be him writing away – neatly (laughs). Now let's see – now I'll think about this: 'Between trees, and warily a lame' . . . (pause). It kind of started out slow and things . . . and really kind of felt, and then it came pssshhh, spread out right into the story, I guess – widening.

Readers may again notice how Carol reads the poem as a whole, looking for patterns and relationships. And it is here she begins to set parallels between the movements of the fox and the movement of images and ideas in the writer's mind. And as she reads on, some of her earlier observations begin to fall into place and others are discarded.

Yeah, a story, I guess. Not just a . . . well, I don't know. 'A widening, deepening' . . . yes . . . (pause). Well, I still don't see the connection of the fox dying . . . (sighs).

Carol's developing account of the poem cannot accommodate her hypothesis that the fox is shot in the head. The interviewer asks if she has decided the fox dies.

Well, what else could 'sudden sharp hot stink of fox' and him do? 'It enters the dark hole of the head.' Ooooooohhh! (laughs) . . . Maybe he's . . . now to become real – his imagination – so he's smelling a fox, and it comes into his mind, as you know, *there*. Yep, and he's not, he's not lonely any more. The clock ticks but it's not lonely any more; 'cause he's got it, he's got his story or his (??) . . . the fox.

As she considers the question of what might have happened to the fox, Carol seems to have made a breakthrough with the realization that the 'sharp hot stink of fox' represents the moment and the act of the fox becoming real. That line no longer supports the notion of the fox having been shot. She also makes a connection with the 'loneliness' she had sensed earlier. The interviewer asks what she means by 'gets'.

On the page and then . . . he's kind of . . . you know you can have imagination but you can also have like, real imagination, like you can feel everything you've . . . and that's what he's kind of . . . he can smell a fox now. . . . So it's become real – for him. [The interviewer urges her to keep talking.] And he's writing a letter, and he's . . . (pause). 'The clock ticks, / The page is printed.' He's written the page and he's written about a fox.

The interviewer asks what happens at the end.

(After a long pause) He's come out of the imagination or [out of] that [which] he felt . . . Oh, wait a minute. He's come out . . . and everything is the same except, he's not lonely any more . . . He's thought of the fox.

The interviewer reads the poem once more and asks if Carol has any final thoughts on the poem.

> This person just created the fox in his mind to keep him away from loneliness – I guess, this is like a friend or something . . . I don't know.

The interviewer asks what 'the page is printed' has to do with this mental creation of the fox. Her response after a while is that the page represents his mind.

Readers may have noticed that the poem has had several readings during the course of this protocol, a few more than were called for in the other two protocols. It seems as though Carol prefers to read the poem as a whole, so that she can consider the meanings of smaller units within the larger context. Implicit also in her RAP is Carol's concern to relate the pattern of events in the poem to human reality. The poet is lonely, the imagined fox becomes real enough to relieve loneliness. Again one might have noticed how she finds parallels between the fox's movements and the completion of the 'story': starting out slowly and widening/deepening into completion.

The pattern of Carol's reading in her other RAPs fits in with 'allegorizing'. Her reading of 'The Thought-Fox' is not noticeably in that pattern of reading, simply because she has concentrated on establishing the pattern of events in the poem. But she has recognized all along aspects of the extended metaphor that the poem is, especially the parallels between the act of writing and the movement of the fox; e.g. '"Neat prints" can be him writing away – neatly.' She asks quite early, for instance, whether the fox is a symbol for anything. One of the characteristics of this pattern of reading is to rely on one's sense of what is happening, and again, early in the RAP, Carol announces that what she knows is that 'something happens to the fox and the person is left as he began', except, as she realizes near the end, 'he is not lonely anymore'. Carol has also been foxlike, stalking the poem in narrowing circles, until she has realized the poem.

Ralph

Ralph is 16 years old, interested in motorbikes and in reading about them. He plans to enter an engineering college.

> (After the interviewer has read the poem) – I think it's a . . . well, this is a bit outrageous but I think it could be a blind person . . . well, oh I know where I got that from: 'And this blank page where my fingers move', reading the braille; and also I thought it could be a blind person because . . . the way it's describing it here, a normal person would read the book, yeah, and . . . think about it as they are reading it, but a blind person would have to read it and imagine it because they haven't got eyes of their own so they can't really say. So that they're all, they imagine it, maybe doesn't even know what a fox is. . . . No, he must know what a fox is, I . . . think, because then 'a fox's nose

touches a twig'; but he could have got that out of a book. He could have got 'dark snow' out of a book. . . . But I think it could be a blind person reading a book and imagining what's happening as he or she sits alone in their house . . . (pause). But this bit, 'The page is printed', throws me off.

On the basis of one reading Ralph has already advanced a hypothesis, albeit tentatively. He tests this notion against what he knows about blind people and what is offered in the poem and recognizes a possible discrepancy that 'throws him off'. Ralph is also able to monitor his own reading: he recognizes what aspects of the text contribute to his understanding. ('I know where I got that from.') He decides to read the poem silently. As he reads, he inquires whether braille readers sound out what is printed in braille. The interviewer says he is not sure. Ralph is encouraged to say what he is thinking.

Well I am trying to match up the [the meaning I am working out]. It matches with the first bit, the blind person, because of the 'blank page where my fingers move'. Now a . . . blind people have to, you know, pick up braille with their fingertips; that's why I thought it was a blind person. 'Through the window I see no star': so maybe . . . maybe she can't see the star 'cause she is blind. 'Something more near / Though deeper within the darkness is entering the loneliness': . . . Maybe she's just, or maybe she can see and she's looking out of the window into the darkness and sees this through deeper within darkness. She's looking or she thinks she's looking through the darkness, and she can see something entering the loneliness. She's calling it loneliness, because it's, you know, it's so dark you can't see anything.

Again one is aware of Ralph's monitoring his own reading. He continues to test the braille–blindness hypothesis, and finds some support in 'see no star'; however, the next line suggests the speaker is watching. He misreads 'though' as 'through', with the result that he sees the viewer as somehow penetrating the darkness. But again he is aware of the alternative: 'She *thinks* she's looking through'. He goes on:

'Cold, delicately as the dark snow' . . . so she's saying that it moves with the delicacy of the snow. When it falls on the ground, it's not a thud, it's soft and delicate. 'A fox's nose touches [a] twig, leaf': that's probably the animal that she is imagining is out there, and is moving delicately. 'Two eyes serve a moment [misreads 'movement'] that now and again now and now': well I don't really know about this bit. 'Two eyes serve [as] a movement' . . . 'Two eyes serve a movement': I think . . . does she mean . . . oh, I think she means to serve a movement, to recognize a movement, I think – that's what that could be . . . that the fox is seeing a movement . . . softly come towards or softly walking around outside 'cause it says it 'sets neat prints in[to] the snow / Between trees and warily a lame' . . . 'Warily a lame' . . . what's 'warily'?

Ralph does not ignore the effects of the images in the poem. He sets aside what he does not understand; he can always return to it later. He experiments with the text, tries out 'serve a movement' against 'serve as a movement'. The interviewer tells him that warily means 'being quite careful'.

> 'Wary', yeah. . . . 'Shadow lags by . . . (pause). Of a body that is bold to come' means that the animal she's describing is a fairly . . . fairly bold animal. I don't know whether this [is] bold or whether it's curiosity, because a fox, I think, is more curious than . . . bold because they don't stay if they see anything that's around bigger than them or of a threat, they don't stay; so I think it's more curiosity than bold . . . 'Across clearings an eye, . . . deepening greenness . . . (pause). A widening deepening greenness': well, I don't know where she gets that greenness from. 'Brilliantly, concentratedly . . . (pause) coming about its own business' . . . I don't understand that bit at all; it really throws me off . . . (pause). . . . And this: 'enters the dark hole of the head' . . . (pause) . . . Oh oh, could be his . . . this is another idea.

Ralph questions the text, often in terms of his own experience. The fox's behaviour in the poem is more to do with curiosity than boldness. Again, Ralph recognizes areas of difficulty but does not let them hold up inquiry. So he gets another idea:

> It could be she's an author, and she – 'the blank page where my fingers move' – she can't think of anything to write, you see, and she wants this bit in the book, and she looks through the window and she – you know she looks through a window and imagines seeing it – and she is thinking of all these things, and she suddenly thinks of the fox, 'cause she probably is thinking what's out there, you know – what could be out there sort of thing – and she thinks of the fox and then she puts all these ideas together: and a 'body that is bold to come', 'eyes serve a movement', she's all, she's putting all this together. You know she's looking right through the window as if she's looking through a . . . a . . . magic sort of window; she's looking through into what she wants to write sort of thing; and she can see it out there, and she's . . . sort of thinking she's putting all these ideas together, you know, across clearings, she can see out there. She can see anything she wants to in her imagination out there until, 'with a sudden sharp hot stink of fox it enters the dark hole of the head': so that all goes into her head now, all these ideas that she has seen through the window; it's all locked in her head now.

It is probably the kind of attention that Ralph pays to the poem (for instance, his noting what he knows and what he is not sure of, his seeing the poem as a whole, his overall tentative stance) that provides the ground for the realizations that now begin to occur. In just the previous segment he had admitted to being stumped by 'enters the dark hole of the head'. But because he does not try to break the code at the local level but considers instead the overall situation, such puzzling phrases begin to make sense. It is as though Ralph were working on a jigsaw puzzle and working out what the subject of the puzzle might be before deciding how some of the more difficult pieces will fit. But that is where the analogy ends, for poems are not merely jigsaw puzzles.

A point worth considering is Ralph's resorting to approximations in what seem to us particularly productive ways. When he says, for instance, that the poet is looking out with the attitude of 'what could be out there, sort of thing', he describes a stance of a watcher that helps explain why the writer thinks of a fox somewhere out there. What is also remarkable is Ralph's ability to plot the situation, exemplified particularly well in his notion of 'a magic sort of window'. He continues to think aloud:

> She looks right through the window, right down, and then this end bit, 'enters the dark hole of the head. / The window is starless still': now she's come back . . . out of her imagination, out of this sort of magic world behind the window. She's come back and she's withdrawn like a zoom lens and she's on the window again, 'cause it says here, 'The window is starless still'. She's back where she started from . . . the first . . . she was looking at the window and now and then she went through it, and now she's come back. She's still looking at the window and the clock ticks, which is another thing to say she's back where she was because it says here, 'Besides the clock's loneliness' and she is back where she was. 'The page is printed' means she's got the ideas and she's writing it down – she's wrote it – the page is then set; that's it. The page is set now. That's what I thought.

What is striking here is Ralph's command of the scenario, particularly in terms of how it relates to the text. Just as striking is his resorting to images to register his understandings: the magic window in the preceding segment, and now the zoom lens. The interviewer asks Ralph to explain how he came to this account of the poem.

> I think . . . (sighs) 'the page is printed', 'the blank page where my fingers move', first of all that's a gesture [indication?] it wasn't a blind person, but then you can't read. That was a first impression, but that threw me off 'the page is printed'. Now if she's got a blank page, and the page is printed, it means she's obviously done something in between that, isn't it? She's had some ideas and she's . . . is now printed. Therefore she must have wrote it down and it just sort of all clicked and I thought, 'Hey, you know she could be an author, is writing a story, and she wants the page to write here, but she hasn't got any ideas. And then she looks through this sort of window or a window of a house into her imagination and sees all these ideas form – you know, the green grass and the fox, the twig, you know, the fox is moving delicately like the snow and all this sort of thing.'

Ralph's account is consistent with the way he has proceeded in the protocol and further evidence of his awareness of his own processes, what cognitive psychologists have called metacognitive awareness. The interviewer asks if 'other things now fall into place'.

> It all sort of fits the description because . . . [Ralph then proceeds through the text in the light of the new understanding he has just announced. We pick

up the text when he gets to line 8.] 'Is entering the loneliness', the loneliness is her blank mind because she's got nothing to write; she's sitting there thinking, Hmmm, I got nothing to write, sort of thing and that's all blank out there. She's got no ideas and then all of a sudden she explains the idea of something creeping in. Yeah, it's entering the loneliness, there is something, some ideas creeping into her mind and 'cold, delicately as the dark snow', is coming in slowly. You know this idea and then all of a sudden 'a fox's nose touches twig, a leaf' – this is the idea starting to form; it's coming into the picture and then she sort of builds up an image around it: the twigs, the leaf. So this is starting to form now, . . . and from the 'two eyes' down to 'of a body that is bold to come' right down to 'coming about its own business' is explaining . . . her ideas, the idea she is thinking of the way it's walking, you know this is the idea, the image.

Ralph manages to align the lines of the poem with the notion of an idea taking shape in the poet's mind. He does not venture beyond saying that the idea that has emerged is the idea of the fox. But he clearly senses parallels between the movements of the fox and the emergence of an idea in writing. He continues to look at the poem and this time is wondering where in the poem the image actually begins to enter the writer's mind.

I think of her blank mind; I think then the image starts to form from 'cold, delicately'; from there rather than from [the following line] 'a fox's nose'. . . . As she explains the movement . . ., you know she's imagining that (pause).

To conclude this part of the RAP, the interviewer asks Ralph if the title of the poem was significant in any way.

'The thought-fox' implies that it's not a real fox; therefore it must be something she has made up, thought.

Ralph's pattern of reading resembles the problem-solving pattern. He is tentative in his approach, considers several hypotheses, draws on his personal experience, and consciously monitors his own reading. Particularly remarkable about this RAP is the concertedness of the effort and the sustained talk, with little or no urging to think aloud.

So what?

These four readers, all in the same class, demonstrate possibilities of meaning and a range of strategies prompting one to ask how such differences might be taken account of in classroom practice. It is unlikely that pupils in a teacher-directed class read poems in many of the ways suggested by these readers. They have seldom, if at all, had the kind of invitation these readers are responding to. They are more likely to read in ways modelled by teachers' questions and procedures. As much classroom observation has shown, pupils soon learn what is expected of them and perform accordingly.

The RAPs are a reminder of possibilities, of actual potential. Thus we might wish to consider, as in Chapter 5, the kinds of practices and the classroom contexts that tap and promote such possibilities. The RAP procedure is in itself an instance of the directions in which classroom practice must move. What in the situation allows readers to speak at such length and with such a high degree of commitment about their transactions with a poem? For one, the situation is non-judgemental; readers are not on trial. Interviewer and pupil are engaged in a context where the interviewer has announced an interest in the pupil's ways of making meaning and the pupil is in the position of informing the listener. There is no search for right answers, exploratory talk is valued, and the pupil is free to review and revise. The frequent re-readings of the poem are themselves an unlikely event in many classrooms. And what is most striking is the amount of talk that is invited and must be allowed for if the reader is to be fully engaged by and with the poem. Thus the RAPs are a challenge: fairly unsophisticated readers of poetry, given the goals they set themselves, are able to engage in fairly sophisticated transactions with a complex poem.

Where readers are limited is primarily in the set of expectations they bring to the task of reading a poem. A lack of appropriate prior knowledge to bring to a poem is not as severe a constraint as one might think. These protocols also point to likely sources of misinterpretation in poetry; for instance, how early impressions from reading a poem lodge in the mind and are hard to displace even when new information is presented.

One must remember of course that these readers had participated earlier (a year earlier in this case) in ten days of the small-group discussion procedure described in Chapter 3. Despite the passage of a year, they had sufficient confidence in their abilities as readers of poetry to accept without hesitation the invitation to think aloud about a poem they had seen for the first time. That they had the resources within themselves to make sense of a poem on their own was the one expectation they held in common. However, as their RAPs show, they differ considerably in how they perceive their task as readers of poetry. Somehow classroom practice must take account of the differing expectations and resources brought to poetry. The theory and research discussed in earlier chapters point the way to practices that can tap such potential.

5 Responsibilities

'Responsibilities' is rather a portentous title for a chapter, but the common origin of the words 'response', 'sponsor' and 'responsibilities' is worth a brief thought. *Spondere* is the Latin for 'to make a promise', with notions of being committed to a task in alliance with others. Earlier chapters have set out to discuss two sources of information for the 'teacher' of poetry – the work of literary and reading theoreticians and the work of researchers seeking to find out at least something of what goes on in adolescents as they engage with poetry. This chapter aims to explore some of the implications of this information for the teacher and to describe some approaches which sponsor pupils as they assume increasing responsibility for their reflective responses to poetry.

'Sponsorship' is sometimes taken to mean the teacher acting on behalf of the pupils in choosing content and approach. There may be the occasion when this well-intentioned intervention is justified, but it is the other meaning of the word that we want to focus on here – 'to support strongly'. How do teachers support strongly their pupils so that they do the growing into increasing confidence and competence as responders to poems? How do teachers help pupils create the sense of being within the exploratory alliance which is suggested by 'responsibility' and which has been implicitly championed elsewhere in this book?

The chapter on research has suggested that pupils are most likely to go on a genuine quest with a poem when they are responsible for that quest, with their wise adult of a teacher an ally, recessive and supportive in manner and tone. Some would argue that the process of at least partly 'achieving' a poem is made even more powerful when the poem has been chosen by the pupil or pupils. How far do such contentions fit with the practice in some classrooms of assuming that the adult must act on behalf of the pupils throughout – must act on their behalf in selecting what shall be read, for instance? What is the effect on a hoped-for collaborative alliance when it is the teacher who chooses the agenda of which poem shall be 'taught' and of which of its features shall be attended to? Often, student teachers note in their teaching files that a class held a discussion about a poem. It takes some courage for them to explore what that discussion involved and to come to terms with the recognition that it bore little resemblance to the discussion about a poem they would have held in other places and other circumstances. The honest and courageous come to recognize that such discussion tends to be a series of dialogues which involve the teacher all the time and single pupils some of the time, with pupils being switched on and off as talkers and being expected to act as attentive listeners throughout the process. 'The Bullock Report' (1975) produced a salutary diagram of a 'good' class discussion in which it was sadly clear that few pupils spoke at any length and that most pupils said nothing at all. Even those who had spoken had, for the most part, been 'reactive', responding to initiatives by the teacher rather than 'pro-active', having the confidence or the desire to say something for themselves. In other words, most of the pupils were made dumb. In such 'discussion' there was no evidence of most of the pupils engaging in any form of alliance other than that of polite silence.

For some pupils, all too often the choice of how to shape and make public their response to poetry is made for them through worksheet or teacher-directed discussion. Many come to perceive these question and answer approaches as a modification of 'Anything you say may be taken down and used in evidence'. The modifications are significant. First, the right to silence is usually denied. Secondly, 'say' is often replaced by 'write'. Thirdly, the notion of 'anything' with its hint of variety and personal choice is often replaced by requests for answers to pre-set questions to which the teacher already knows the answers. In Britain, there is still a tendency to place a premium on the well-wrought essay. In some North American systems, the premium placed on the question paper with its demands for focused answers is equally constraining.

What do teachers do when they wish to avoid imposing content, approach and means of expression on their pupils? In spite of the 1987 unease of Her Majesty's Inspectorate in England and Wales that poetry teaching is in a questionable state, there are teachers who see themselves as sponsors in that second sense, of being wise adults who 'support strongly'. They are wise enough to know that this strong support can range from setting up ritualized exploratory behaviour to that strongest of all support, letting go.

Responsibilities for poems

A teacher has as much right as anyone else to bring a poem into a classroom – but not more. The quiet enthusiast who creates a classroom climate in which anyone, pupil or teacher, can introduce a poem, read it and leave it in the air is bearing witness to an important point for some pupils – that everyone is equally prepared to take risks about poetry, to be vulnerable, and that everyone should be equally prepared to be supportive of one another. Creating a classroom which provides for such informal presentations as part of its 'poetry climate' takes time, but it can be done. Implicit in that approach are two theses: that everyone has something to give; that everyone has obligations and rights to share it. As Ingham showed (1981), the classroom in which everyone believed they had the right to contribute and to 'gossip' – to discuss and respond informally and non-judgementally – was the classroom in which further reflectiveness and literary insight could grow.

Such openness depends on extensive, relaxed familiarity with poetry – lots of it – which means that pupils must have the right to browse. While much of this chapter will look at the potential of interpretive communities, it is worth remembering that there is room for privacy in education as well. Josipovici (1977) suggested that there are two basic approaches to literature – 'silence' and 'game'. 'Games' involving collaboration will be constantly referred to in the rest of this book, so it is worth establishing now a pupil's other right, to engage in an interpretive community with a poet or a poem without involving other people. Josipovici's 'silence' is an essentially active process which expects us as teachers to be aware of its going on and sponsoring it – supporting it strongly – by keeping out until we are invited in.

Browsing can also be carried out as a communal activity. For example, there is the classroom which sets up paired browsing very much within Ingham's philosophy of promoting sharing, experiment, and evaluation without anyone being called to account. Younger classes in secondary education may have time set aside on a regular basis for relaxation. Pupils can be allocated 20 minutes in which to relax with poetry, the only obligation being to read silently for a while and then to read to one another and chat about what has been read. The device is simple. It requires clear explanation of its rules – that this is a time for a degree of quietness; that people are sharing poems and views in pairs; that this is a time to relax, experiment and explore, using one's partner as a sounding board about one's choices and opinions. It is a good initial means of getting pupils to take responsibility for their own choices and tastes; it is equally useful for those teachers who need time in which to get rid of their Calvinist belief that recessiveness in a teacher is a professional sin. The pupils are learning, in a small environment, about how to make choices of their own. They are also learning how to teach one another as they work out how to respond to the poems and responses of their partners. A formal class of, say, 30 pupils, has become 15 attempts at peer tutoring at a very basic level, providing the teacher with a rich opportunity to observe and perceive some of the tastes and tactics which are the pupils' own.

A third stage in the process of helping pupils to make their own choice of poems comes when they make decisions about poems which they wish to explore further. The suggestion has already been made that there will be times when some pupils will want to do so privately and as soloists. There are two other options of which they should be aware, both based on interpretive communities. One is for pairs or small groups to choose poems which they wish to continue to engage with more fully. The other is for groups to identify poems which they believe the rest of the class should encounter. This last approach has problems. How is it different from when poems are chosen by the teacher? How is the content handled differently? The partial answer is that the content has been chosen by peers; they are its immediate sponsors, not the adult. As for choice of approach, if the pupils have encountered at least some of the range described in the rest of this chapter and elsewhere, they are likely to be involved in working out which ones might be appropriate for their materials. It is possible for a teacher to commission each 'pupil consortium' in a classroom to find poems for attention later in the term or semester. Each can be given some time out of class time to discuss what it sees as appropriate methods of presentation and response and to present these to the teacher as a lesson proposal. If it is necessary to do so, the teacher comes in at this stage as a consultant, helping a group refine and develop what it proposes should happen. For instance, if a group decides to present the poem as a taped group reading, it may want the teacher as friendly critic to listen to it before it becomes the object of class discussion. If it decides that the poem is an appropriate one for others to filmscript or for some form of dramatization, it may want to discuss who should be in charge of the lesson's control. The consortium is responsible for the poem and preparing for its classroom life. The teacher has been the consortium's consultant – its attentive but non-interventionist sponser.

There is one further point to make about providing for extensive browsing in poetry. When it comes to working with prose texts, many schools provide for silent, solo and class reading and for reading in small groups. For example, the 'theme box' approach has meant that in many classrooms you will find pupils reading alone or in twos, threes or fours, according to the texts they have chosen from the variety in the box. There might be four copies of each of half a dozen books, two each of others and a few single copies of those likely to require private reading or to attract only a small clientele. In contrast, many schools invest only in class sets of poetry books. There is a case for providing half sets, so that by sharing texts everyone can join in celebrating poems as a community from time to time. But the exclusive use of one book denies access to others. The sorts of browsing argued for so far, from the private and perhaps aimless to the shared and definitely focused, require an adaptation of the 'book box' approach. There should be as many poetry books as a school can afford – poetry posters, with their appeal to the eye as well – tapes or records of poets and other voices making poems in sound – the words of lyrics and their realization on records and videos. Poetry is interpreted and celebrated in many ways. As far as finances and organization will allow, pupils should have access to these as part of the positive climate for poetry in their school. Links with local public libraries and borrowing through inter-school networks or from local educational resource centres can help to enrich what is available for pupils to taste and choose. All of us can dream of the ideal world in which copyright has been outlawed and intelligent computers track and print poems without fuss! In the actual world, reality's constraints need not entirely sabotage efforts to produce rich and varied sources of poetry.

Towards the collegial

'Colleague' has two origins, one meaning to choose to work together and the other to join in an alliance. According to the *Shorter Oxford Dictionary*, a 'college' is not to do with ancient bricks and mortar but people – 'an organised society of persons performing certain common functions and possessing special rights and privileges'. That may not sound like some classrooms! Nevertheless, what it is positing is an ideal in which a community does meet to work together within 'systems' which safeguard itself and its rights to learn. How to produce a climate in which pupils will work as colleagues, in 'colleges'? Nobody knows for sure, but there are approaches which are worth exploring.

We want to suggest that Bruner's (1966) notion of three means of interpreting the world gives us one practical, simple set of items against which to check possible approaches. Without traducing his commentary too grossly, it is worth thinking of (1) the *enactive*, (2) the *iconic* and (3) the *symbolic* as (1) physically acting things out, (2) visually processing them and (3) exploring–expressing them through verbal language. Much of this chapter will argue for having pupils use language to explore the role language plays in poems – but it is possible to rely too much on language and to use it only for certain fairly detached forms of commentary, such as the literary critical essay and the advanced seminar. There is a place for these at senior level, but there should be places for the enactive and iconic and for other roles for the symbolic as well.

One other writer can be of some common sense use. Barthes (1974) suggested that readers pay attention to five 'codes' in exploring a text and partly occupying it. He suggests that the text 'braids' these as it needs them – and implies that we do the same. The five can be summed up a little simplistically as:

1 *The semic*: coping with what words and phrases literally mean, and their connotations and implications.
2 *The symbolic*: seeing what the text is about – its motif or theme.
3 *The proairetic*: exploring what happens – interaction between the text and the reader as the reader sets up expectations and 'intelligent guesses'.

4 *The hermeneutic*: exploring the hidden meanings in the text – the role of the implied and even unstated in a text.
5 *The referential*: using references to knowledge which the writer assumes the reader will already have.

Each of these codes assumes active readers – that they will be ready to be responsive to the 'tremulations' of sense typical of connotative language; that they will ask questions and explore what a poem might be in the process of generating an overall but provisional 'meaning'; that they will engage in 'intelligent guessing'; that they will cope with and even enjoy the problematic nature of the text, with its hints and clues and silences; that they will bring their life experiences with them to the text and be prepared to engage in sharing them and, sometimes, furthering them through discussion and scholarship, in order to engage more fully with the poem.

If we are prepared to accept these two related notions: Bruner's, that learning is fundamentally active and Barthes's, that a reader must be active in meeting the activity of a text, then we impose certain obligations when it comes to pedagogy. As Reid (1984) has said in Australia, our task is to promote a workshop approach to poetry, not that of a reverential visit to a museum. Reid sees his workshops as cooperative groups. We agree, seeing them as occasions for working as colleagues – hence our term for such groups, 'colleges', which is intended to suggest the seriousness with which we should treat them and the learning which should go on through them. Seriousness does not imply solemnity or silence: there is likely to be quite a lot of energy and quite a lot of argument! As Milton once said of another reformation: 'Where there is much desire to learn, there of necessity will be much arguing, much writing, many opinions; for opinion in good men is but knowledge in the making.'

The enactive

Unless they have had experience of improvisation, many adolescents become self-conscious at the thought of taking a poem and acting it out in some way. Some also find difficulty in dealing with enacting poetry since often it turns away from clear narrative. Unlike conventional stories, many poems celebrate another 'primary act of mind', an attitude or emotion. They create and reflect upon recollected events and feelings through what has been called the *spectator* role. Trying to impose the enactive in these circumstances can all too easily create unease and self-consciousness.

Nevertheless, if improvisation is seen as a means of 'sketching out' ideas – as a provisional activity leading to further work rather than as performance – it is occasionally possible to harness the enactive. At its simplest, action can grow from group discussion – small 'colleges' of pupils identifying the potential in a poem and working out how it can be expressed. It is possible to start with narrative poems. Their storyline gives pupils a structure to hold on to and, if the poems are long enough, each college can adopt a section and look after its production, while negotiating some degree of continuity of approach with the other colleges. 'How are we going to say our section?', 'How are we going to move it?', and 'What special effects do we need?' are questions of the poem and of themselves, leading from the tentative and debative to a product which contributes to a continuing discussion, rather than being a closure, an end in itself.

When sponsoring enactive work, encourage and support divergence in choice of poem and of interpretation. Some colleges might want to remain as loyal as possible to a poem's actual text. Some might find that the words start to get in the way of any fluent improvisation and decide to read the poem first and then present their interpretation as a linked but independent item. Some might want to use the poem as a springboard from which to create a plausible narrative and then go on to dramatize that instead. Some groups choose to involve their full membership; some prefer to act as small theatres, identifying their 'best' voices and actors who are then directed by the rest of the team. Again, the pupils are questioning the poem as well as themselves as they work out how they will read and enact what they have created from its text.

Where to start? There are many modern narrative poems, but old ballads can be useful. Their terse narratives often provide sufficient framework for improvisatory exploration to take place – and leave enough of Iser's 'gaps' for some problem-solving and conjecture to be needed as well. Best of all are those which read almost as a play script such as the old Scottish ballad, 'Edward'. What is the implied pre-story? How far shall it be part of the improvisation? How is a whole college to be involved when the text has only two voices? Shall it be read faithfully in Mediaeval Scots or modernized? Is this poem best 'done live' or as a tape, in which the voices will have to do all the acting? And so the questions go on as each college tackles that bitter ballad with its stark opening.

> Why does your brand sae drop wi' blude,
> Edward, Edward?
> Why does you brand sae drip wi' blude,
> And why sae sad gang ye, O?' –
> 'O I hae kill'd my hawk sae gude,
> Mither, Mither,
> O I hae kill'd my hawk sae gude,
> And I had nae mair but he, O.

More recent ballads are one source of material. So are the many folk songs which have arisen from the people over centuries in Britain, Ireland, North America, Australia, the West Indies and elsewhere, with their stories of love and hate, of social struggle, of protest. So are many recent and current popular songs, from a country and western to a protest song, if we accept that poetry does not have to confine itself to notions of some exclusivist forms of high literature. So are some narrative poems. For example, the tension between the protagonists in the dialogue of 'Edward' is present for a different reason as a black in search of a room tackles a white landlady in Wole Soyinka's 'Telephone Conversation':

> 'ARE YOU DARK? OR VERY LIGHT?' Revelation came.
> 'You mean – like plain or milk chocolate?'
> Her assent was clinical, crushing in its light
> Impersonality. Rapidly, wavelength adjusted,
> I chose, 'West African sepia' – and as an afterthought,
> 'Down in my passport.' Silence for spectroscopic
> Flight of fancy, till truthfulness changed her accent
> Hard on the mouthpiece. 'WHAT'S THAT?' conceding
> 'DON'T KNOW WHAT THAT IS.' 'Like brunette.'

Senior colleges will find interpreting the commentary in that poem as stage directions quite a challenge. They will find taking on other narrative poems equally problematic. For instance, Robert Frost's lovely 'Paul's Wife' raises the matter of how to cope with length and the poem's extensive use of commentary and pre-story as well as the more delicate issue of how to recreate its elegaic mood and tone. On a more sardonic note, 'archy is shocked' by Don Marquis is an occasion for fun as a dignified old man on a crowded subway train:

> suddenly reached up and
> pulled his own left eye
> from the socket and ate it

The reactions of the rest of the car give an opportunity for legitimate melodrama, and the arguments between the old man and the 'wise boid' of a guard contain several insights to interpret and present. In sum, there are many poems available for colleges to play with, as Harris and McFarlane's (1985) collection for the Australian Association for the Teaching of English, *A Book to Perform Poems By*, so enthusiastically shows.

Given appropriate training in it as a resource, some colleges choose to work through mime. This requires a lot of confidence and can involve the teacher in being quite firm about the climate of response, but it has the advantage of freeing everyone from having to rely exclusively on narrative poems. The lovely Navajo Beautyway Healing Chant provides an opportunity for antiphonal reading and movement to go with it:

> In beauty   may I walk
> All day long   may I walk
> Through the returning seasons   may I walk
> Beautifully will I possess again
> Beautifully birds

> Beautifully joyous birds
> On the trail marked with pollen may I walk

and so on.

The Sumerian cry of a poem 'The Seven', with its dread and hatred caught in its repetition of words and images, lends itself to far more powerful movement.

> They are 7 in number, just 7
> In the terrible depths they are 7
> Bow down, in the sky they are 7

This can be read by a few voices while others mime it, but other colleges have made this poem their own by involving everyone in the reading and in its movement. For example, one group chose to be an inchoate, silent, formless group on the floor. A hissing sound repeating the one word 'seven, seven, seven', slowly grew into a hunched, inward-facing group from which one face at a time dared to turn and whisper the first line. And so the interpretation went on, as the group used its bodies as an extension of its voices.

It can be argued that the mouth is a theatre in miniature in which we physically enact a poem in terms of sound. The tongue is aware of textures, pressures and movements as it collaborates in taking a poem from its silence on the page and makes it into sound. The fixed print becomes a dynamic of volume, pitch, pace, cadence, texture, tone, pause, silence. This is language being used to celebrate, an interface between Bruner's enactive and symbolic.

At its simplest, this is to be found in the paired browsing described earlier, in which pupils simply read poems or bits of poems to one another. Often, those readings will be as undemonstrative as the chatting which accompanies them – a kind of tentative, not too committed, exploratory swapping of poems which might possibly be followed up at some time. That is fine and should be encouraged as much as possible. From it can grow those occasions when a poem is chosen for further exploration as a live reading or, with its even greater focus on sound, a tape. Shy young colleges often retreat to a tape, but seniors come to know that a taped reading is not an easy option, for the sound has to be so active and carry so much of the interpretation. One college set out to produce an anthology of poems on cats, weaving its own with those it found in books and trying to weave in cat sounds as well. A college of third-year (13- and 14-year-old) boys who were not noted for their literary enthusiasm decided to make an anthology of poetry and prose about war, using one member's budding skills as a drummer to provide atmosphere. The tape began by celebrating bravura warfare with the drums providing quantities of machine guns, mortars and heavy bombs – all very macho – but, as the browsing for printed material continued and as conversations with adults told of the unheroic side of war, the project was revised. Poems found themselves in the company of soldier and civilian anecdotes; poetry about refugees and against war existed alongside recruiting documents; the drums and the voices had more roles to assume and express than anyone in the college had ever thought of when they first set out. By adult standards, the resulting tape was technically crude; the collaborative exploration needed for its creation was not.

Anthologies are one way of exploiting this celebratory use of the voice, but single poems can be equally effective, especially for senior pupils. Sylvia Plath's 'The arrival of the bee box' is a classic challenge for older colleges to interpret, with its complex of demands. Consider her reaction to the bees and how this verse might be rendered on tape:

> How can I let them out?
> It is the noise that appals me most of all,
> The unintelligible syllables.
> It is like a Roman mob,
> Small, taken one by one, but my god, together!

Even more challenging is a poem which demands only one reader, for the college must support its soloist carefully. Even an ostensibly light poem can set such a challenge, as the Canadian poet Paulette Jiles shows in her 'Time to Myself', which starts:

> It takes time to make
> yourself a stranger.
>
> I go through town unknowing
> all the people I have met.
>
> Hands unshake themselves, glances
> miss each other,
> > I take back reams of words.

The English poet and verse speaker Oliver Bernard has exploited the demands imposed by such poetry to create genuine collegiality. Colleges can work upon their own choice of poems, but this device is also an occasion for exploring the same poem, in order to see how interpretations differ. The technique relies upon a set ritual. As Dias's work has shown, where pupils see some point to them, they adopt and internalize these protocols pretty quickly and having a range to choose from increases their sense of competence and independence.

Pupils form themselves into colleges – usually about four to a college. The rules are simple. Everyone reads the poem quietly and privately, deciding how to read it out loud. Ideally, everyone has a copy of the poem which can be annotated, so that each person knows when she or he wants to read loudly or quietly, wants to pause, have a gentle voice or a rough one, and so on.

Then each member reads the poem to the rest of the college and the others listen, seeking out features and items in the reading which they like. If necessary, they can ask a reader to read those pieces again. After each reading, the other members discuss it in positive terms, saying what they particularly liked, were intrigued by, found challenging, etc. So it goes on, until every member of the college has read the poem to the others. Already, the poem has been visited several times and its soundings commented on supportively. When the process works well, certain points are likely to be held in common; some will show signs of differentiation and even disagreement. In all cases, the comments are expected to be linked to a reason. 'I liked that bit where your voice went quiet, because . . .'.

In the next phase, each college is expected to identify its most appropriate Voice for that particular poem and to rehearse its owner for a plenary reading which will make use of the college's previous readings and insights. Where there is disagreement, the owner of the Voice has final right of interpretation. In the next phase, each Voice reads the poem to the class. In the early days, it is essential that the atmosphere be strongly supportive – a sponsoring one – with other colleges saying what they liked about a reading. Later, it is possible to move into the fourth phase in which teacher and class seek to explore differences of interpretation. 'Your college chose a male voice, but the last two chose female ones. How did anyone think that affected the poem?' 'Our college read the end of the poem sadly but this college has just read it without any sadness at all and we'd like to know why.' The teacher should avoid answering any points him/herself but should make discussion the responsibility of the colleges. The Voices should be allowed to rest; any comments explaining a college's reading should come from its other members, for it is their turn to talk. The teacher's task is to promote a supportive climate which, with senior pupils, becomes an increasingly rigorous but courteous one as well. It is also useful to create a 'temporary terminus' at the end of a session by drawing the class into a review of the learning process so far, so that it sees what it has achieved as well as identifying further points for departure.

The iconic

'Image' and 'imagination' are very close cousins in the dictionary and in the feeling intellect of the poet who, like Wordsworth, first gazes and, later, reflects with the 'inward eye'. That second eye is the one we use in what has been called our *spectator* role. Britton linked that role with his notion of 'poetic' language – language used to create and shape the fictions we use to explore and interpret all that we encounter in our lives. In other words, ideas of poetry and the visual constantly intertwine as we try to explain either.

There is perhaps one further reason why poetry and the visual are so often linked. If you consider a play by Shaw, you will recall how his description of a setting may go on for several pages. However, as the curtain goes up in the theatre almost all that linear description is visually present at once in 'virtual simultaneity', a pattern to be explored as the eye and the mind choose. So it is with most poems. There may be an initial, linear reading but most are brief enough after that to have their lines all on stage at once, again for the eye and mind to work and play with as they choose, creating patterns of significance.

One of the most obvious and yet most problematic tasks we face is finding ways of getting pupils to see that a poem's shape can be an iconic message in itself. Poets have used special formats for years, from George Herbert's appropriately shaped 'Easter Wings' to the experiments of many concrete poets. But in its choice of a particular layout even 'ordinary' poetry can be signalling possibilities. A long, thin poem is likely to be different in pace and tone from one which is short and fat; one which is set out without any visible break is likely to be different from one which has neatly separated, regular blocks of four lines, or one which has an irregular pattern. In a century which has encouraged experiment with layout, pupils should have some awareness of how it can be played with, often through creating and playing with layout themselves. When they encounter a poem, it does not take a minute to half-shut the eyes so that the words become a blur and the shape is momentarily considered in its own right. At a senior level, some pupils enjoy exploring for poems which ignore conventional layouts or, more subtly, subvert them. Consider Robert Graves as he presents his well-behaved 'Poem: A Reminder' on the conventions of poetry which, he says, combine:

> To mean: 'Read carefully. Each word we chose
> Has rhythm and sound and sense. This is not prose.'

Graves presents the same poem differently on the facing page – or a different poem. Those words, for example, appear as

                                                      read
              care
                        -fully each word we chose has

                                  rhythm and
                                  sound and
                                  sense this is
              not prose

Working out collegially a stance to the polite poem and its maverick neighbour is no idle exercise. In their exploitation of contrast, Graves's two versions of one poem – or two poems – raise clear questions for pupils to ask about the nature, purpose and significance of the layout games that poets can play as they write 'notprose'.

Clearly, there are games which pupils can play back. Colleges can adopt conventionally presented poems and create new layouts which, they believe, help to set out the theme, focuses, images and stress patterns sympathetically. Here is an instance of where the word-processor can be useful, enabling a college as an editorial team to work together as it revises the poem's original layout and sets out its own. Discussion will inevitably arise as a college tries to persuade others of the quality of its revision and as the effect of the temporary violence which the exercise has created is assessed by others.

However, this is likely to be too sophisticated for younger forms. Where then should they start? One obvious way is to have pupils try to write visually themselves, from creating naive 'shape' poems or experimenting with layout to writing poems which focus on the visual through extended use of imagery. There are justifiably well known books on harnessing the visual in young peoples' own poetic writing across the world: in America, the work of Kenneth Koch (1973), such as *Rose, Where Did You Get That Red?*; in Britain, the publications of Sandy Brownjohn, such as *Does It Have to Rhyme?* and *Into Poetry* by Richard Andrew; in Australia, Rory Harris and Peter McFarlane's *A Book to Write Poems By*. All of these contain approaches for encouraging the attentive and reflective 'second eye', from writing the brevities of haiku and kennings to creating extended poems. Using the sense of the visual as a means of responding to poems created by other people can be developed in several ways.

One set of approaches clusters around using not only ready-made poems but ready-made visual materials. Younger and less confident pupils may well find some support as they try to explore their response to poetry if they are encouraged to interleave poems and pictures in their personal ring-binder anthologies and to write a few lines about why a particular picture has been placed alongside a poem. The approach can be modified to involve collegiality, as groups are commissioned to produce poetry displays. Younger colleges are likely to produce a paste-up of poems and pictures which is simple in its treatment of a theme and with the pictures obviously faithful to the poems. Senior colleges take little encouragement to be more divergent; to set up tensions among the poems or between the poems and their visual commentary.

One simple, elegant but demanding device is to ask senior pupils to write down as quick impressions the shape of the poem they have just read; the colours they would want to mount it on for display; the texture of the mounting material. Justifying their visual hunches within a group can lead to considerable discussion simply because the initial response to the poem was not allowed to be made safe by language. The iconic has been asked to act in an uncompromising fashion; now, language has to come in, to negotiate, defend and, maybe, accede to others' interpretations of the poem.

There is quite a growth industry in analysing peoples' calligraphy and their doodles. That seems to have little relevance to approaches in which pupils are encouraged to make their own iconic representations as they encounter a poem. The most obvious device is to encourage pupils to look at and listen to a poem and to doodle during their first two or three encounters with it. You may well prefer not to use the word 'doodle' with its possible connotations of triviality and facetiousness, but your description should explain that you are after the half-aware, intuitive illustration rather than something which has been carefully and deliberately thought through. Pupils can then comment on their doodles – or the absence of them – in their notebooks, if they wish to work alone, or can share their drawings and interpretations with others. That is not necessarily a juvenile activity. We have seen it used with higher degree students in the Netherlands and with high-school teachers on both sides of the Atlantic as much as with school pupils. Consider this translation of a Dutch poem, 'Melopee', a lament by Paul van Ostaijen. Read it to yourself quietly, then aloud and go on to see what happens when you draw your impressions of it.

Melopee – for Gaston Burssens

Beneath the moon flows the long river
Beside the long river travels wearily the moon
Beneath the moon on the long river the canoe moves towards the sea.

Beside the tall reeds
Beside the low pastures
The canoe moves towards the sea
Moves with the travelling moon towards the sea.
So, together, seawards go canoe and moon and man.
Why do the moon, the man go meekly together to the sea?

Show the poem to someone else and ask them to read the poem, to listen to you read it and to produce their own illustration, no matter how simple it may be. There will be similarities and differences between your drawings which have not been expressed in words. Now words can come in, to help articulate these initial responses. One variation of this technique is to have people share their drawings in pairs, with each telling the other what he or she sees in the partner's drawing. The interpretations tend not to be facetious and lead to yet further exploration of the poem.

There are more consciously artistic approaches to poetry. One is to commission individuals or groups to produce a picture series to accompany a poem. An obvious if rather long example is a narrative poem, such as Coleridge's 'Rime of the Ancient Mariner'. Various groups can assume responsibility for sections of the poem, if this is approved of. At the plenary, various questions arise. Which illustrator has found what in the poem? How 'faithful' has an illustration been? How far is an illustrator obliged to be 'faithful'? Faithful to what? The questions which arise from such illustrative work move between discussion of the pictures and of the text. They can be left to flourish at inter-group level. If they are to be raised at a class plenary, it may be worth duplicating some of the illustrations or presenting them on an overhead projector. There are times when other artists' interpretations are available. Some of Gustave Doré's classic series of engravings in response to Coleridge's poem can be introduced at this stage for further comment on what similarities and dissimilarities exist between the pupils' and his choice of what to illustrate and how to illustrate it – on what that 'inward eye' told the eye and the hand to do.

This approach need not depend solely on narrative poems. Younger colleges or individuals can produce interesting visions of descriptive mood poems, such as Keats's 'Ode to Autumn', while seniors can produce powerful visual commentary on a poem such as Shakespeare's Sonnet LXXIII, 'That time of year thou mayst in me behold' with its dense images of autumn verging on winter, of late twilight, of a dying fire – and then realize the problems of holding on to the visual as the poem reiterates that these images are to be found in its persona and as it shifts gear in its final couplet. There are times when pupils produce drawings which are worth keeping in their own right. Otherwise, they should be valued for their role in encouraging exploration and expression which have been initially untrammelled by words.

The iconic has one further role to play in helping pupils to explore what a poem can and cannot do. Storyboarding – producing a filmscript for a poem – is an excellent means of promoting collegial investigation of a poem and responses to it. The approach can be as simple or complicated as you wish. A basic form is to provide sheets of paper with film screens printed on them with a few lines under each one. Pupils may well need several of these as they make preliminary sketches of how they will set up a poem as a series of filmic episodes. Rough sketches go in the 'screens', with the appropriate section of the poem and any comments on camera and voice going on the lines beneath. (Senior groups may wish to play with long-shot, full-frame, half-frame, close-up, extreme close-up, track, pan, zoom-in, zoom-out, and so on, but these are not entirely necessary.) What becomes clear, even with simple poems, is that there is no easy visual transposition to a storyboard, no easy translation to what might be a film. Take, for example, this apparently simple poem by the Canadian poet W. W. E. Ross, 'The Snake Trying':

> The snake trying
> to escape the pursuing stick,
> with sudden curvings of thin
> long body. How beautiful
>
> and graceful are his shapes!
> He glides through the water away
> from the stroke. O let him go
> over the water
>
> into the reeds to hide
> without hurt. Small and green

> he is harmless even to children.
> Along the sand
>
> he lay until observed
> and chased away, and now
> he vanishes in the ripples
> among the green slim reeds.

Colleges will soon find problems to cope with. How to start the film? Some start at the beginning of the poem. Some start at the end. One even dismantled the poem to create the actual sequence of events which the poem plays with. How to cope with the moments of commentary? How to create the speed and shock of events for the humans and for the snake? The questions which arise because of the demands of the storyboarding technique become questions about the poem itself. It is probably worth starting this approach with brief poems: Tennyson's 'The Eagle' is a well-known verse for this purpose.

Implicit within this sample of ways of exploiting the iconic are two key notions. One is that, as with the enactive, those ways may be useful in themselves in enabling some pupils to explore poems and to express themselves. The second is to be found in a poem by Robert Graves called 'The Cool Web', a poem which sets out the paradox of our discovering much through language and yet its being a means of labelling, containing, making safe the chaos and flux of reality. There are times when allowing the iconic priority springs surprises, which reliance on words would not have allowed.

The symbolic

Graves's poem ironically warns that language's cool web 'winds us in'. Nevertheless, it is an essential and inevitable skill that we possess and there are times when it may release rather than bind us. Certainly its use has been present in all the approaches to poetry suggested so far. In its flexibility, language probably provides more means of exploring poetry than the other two modes. The rest of this chapter can suggest only a sample of approaches which respect individuals, whether they are working on their own or in small colleges.

It has been suggested that the best way of understanding a language is by using it. So it is with poetry – receiving it and creating it. Certainly, pupils should be encouraged to write poetry, on their own where that is appropriate but also, where it suits, with others. Much 'creative writing' captures spontaneous feeling, the beginnings of Wordsworth's 'emotion recollected in tranquility'. It is to be encouraged inasmuch as it provides the initial phase in experiencing the poet's task of struggling to fuse vision and words, of trying to say the unsayable and using every appropriate trick to do so. But there are extensions from this as pupils come to understand the need to move on from the spontaneous, incorporating it into the reflective and shaped language of a poem.

If we accept the notion that learning is as much caught as taught, so it is that we come to 'learn', come to be wise, about poetry. There can be no enforced system of learning the 'grammars' of poetry, since we cannot say how a poem will set up a relationship with its reader or college of readers. Eliot's 'My words echo thus in your mind' catches the notion of a relationship which has a partial transfer of ownership – and the word 'echo' suggests an unpredictability as to what associations and thoughts the poem will encounter and continue to create in the reader.

One approach to creating a sense of poetry as 'poesis' – shape, form – is to ask pupils to write within verse formulae. For instance, there are many books which set out for pupils the 5–7–5 syllable rules of a Japanese haiku as a device for escaping from conventions of rhyme and rhythm and focusing on image as the main cohesive device. (If anything, that particular device is overworked and is offered to some pupils too early.) Formulae without motivation are sterile. If they are to be used, they should grow out of being moved by poems which employ them already and out of a wish to try the devices for oneself.

There are times when such attempts will be carried out in private – a version of Josipovici's 'silence'. There may also be times when a group may wish to experiment with a form. Exploration of ballads and of some of their themes of heroism, love, betrayal, catastrophe and protest can lead a class to create its own. Each of its sub–groups takes on a stage of the ballad's narrative and is responsible for its being created in agreed ballad form. At the end of the process, the stanzas are strung together to create the complete ballad. The device is an obvious one, relying on a clearly needed regularity of form which makes it ideal for younger adolescent pupils. It has another advantage in that ballads have always been a public form of poetry. They provide a genuine chance for collaborative writing, on paper or on a word-processor – and a chance for plenary discussion, revision and celebration. Older pupils may enjoy wrestling with other verse conventions; at least, if they do not, they have some idea of the sets of rules which a poet has chosen to set up in order to keep all talents and wits alive in creating a poem.

There is room for a slightly looser writing process of 'echoing' a poem. Some pupils will be able to write very close technically to a poem and also echo its tone but many prefer a slightly more forgiving approach in which they are asked to follow a poem's form as best they can but to concentrate on echoing its mood, if necessary using its images and even its language where they cannot create an echo in any other way. The device is a demanding one but, handled fairly lightly and seen as an interim task, it provides experience and material for collegiate discussion about how the original poem was created and what it could (and could not) express that the echo poem has tried to achieve.

A means of combining the formulaic and the echoic with senior students (for example in Britain in the Lower-Sixth or in Canada in the Twelfth Grade) is to set out both. This is a device which should be explored by pupils working in pairs: the aim is not to create great poetry but to investigate the problems of content, lexis and form which confront a poet as matters of choice and even dilemma. Take, for example, Robert Frost's poem 'Stopping By Woods on a Snowy Evening'. The teacher's task is to provide the contents of the poem as a monologue which echoes something of the poem's mood. The monologue can be given live, provided on a tape so that it can be referred to, or, as a last resort, written down. 'You're thinking that you know whose woods these are that you are close to, but he lives in the village and will not be around to see you as you stop to watch his woods and the snow which falls and fills them. The thought crosses your mind that your horse – no great charger this – must wonder what you are up to, stopping away from anywhere, from any farmhouse, here between these woods and that frozen lake on this evening, the darkest of the year.' And so on. 'Your poem has to be in four verses of four lines each. Your first verse ends with your reference to that falling, filling snow. The second ends with that darkest evening in the year.' And so on. 'Your rhyme scheme, if you want to have a go at it, is a tricky one – aaba, bbcb, ccdc, dddd. I'll quite understand if you decide to drop that, but at least try to create one of your own, since the original poem did rhyme.'

The wrestling with lexis and form is fused with the attempt to catch the mood implicit in the poem's re-telling. It is interesting how pairs will struggle with such a task as this, although the less secure may need the teacher's occasional help as a consultant and reassurance that the end-product is not going to be judged. It is, however, going to be published, either by being read aloud or by being duplicated with the poems created by others in the room. As always, the teacher seeks positive comments on what has been achieved, as he/she gets colleges and finally the plenary to focus on the similarities and dissimilarities of expression to be found. Teachers should promote inter-group discussion on what choices had to be made, where lay the constraints, where pairs met insoluble problems and where, from time to time, they felt that they triumphed. It is only after this stage that the other poem, in this instance Robert Frost's, is introduced. The process of exploring Frost's problems, challenges, dilemmas and achievements can now begin without reverence and with proper respect, sometimes for Frost's attempt at creating a poem and sometimes for their own.

Teachers are constantly inventive in finding or developing further tactics. Take as an example Tom McKendy of Marianopolis College, Montreal, and his extension of another means of harnessing some senior pupils' pleasure and talent in creating faithful pastiche. Parody can also be fun, but this device deliberately sets out to be so faithful that there can be problems in sorting out which is the original poem in the Cryptic Triptych. The brave teacher invites pupils to choose the original poem without letting him or her know so that everyone, apart from the writer or writers of the pastiches, is in the dark when a triptych is presented to the class. The triptychs now come into their own as a means of promoting collegial discussion of poetry. Finding the original is often easy, but it is interesting how many times it is very difficult. When the teacher makes the wrong choice, this should be an occasion for wry rejoicing as much as embarrassment. Teachers have rights to be puzzled and to make mistakes about poetry like any other citizen! Take, for instance, these opening lines of the three poems in a cryptic triptych based on Theodore Roethke's 'The Pickle Belt':

> The fruit rolled by all day,
> They prayed the cogs would creep,
> They thought about Saturday pay
> And Sunday sleep.

> Eight 'til six on the pickle belt,
> The fruit would keep on rollin';
> By Saturday they'd all have smelled
> But cleaned for Saturday strollin'.

> The flow of fruit was never-ending;
> Henry Ford would have been proud
> To see assembled fifty backs all bending,
> The cogs a-creaking just too loud.

Some triptychs may well be worth celebrating in their own right, but their main purpose is to generate discussion. Which was the original poem? How do we know? What makes any of these 'poetic'? And so on.

There is the reverse of this technique, in which a college reworks a poem into prose as faithfully as it can; and passes it to another to rework into another version as faithfully as it can; and on to another. This version of Chinese Whispers will again produce material for discussion in which pupils can see what has changed and, maybe has been lost, through these shifts of expression.

Chinese Whispers is an attempt at remaining faithful to the original while coping with imposed and inevitable distortion. There is a version of this to be played orally. Most poems written in England, for example, assume that they will be spoken with some sort of 'English' voice, with its particular accent and cadence. A New England poem assumes that its effectiveness will be at its best when read with a voice from that region. A poem by a man is, perhaps, at its most appropriate when read by a man; written by a woman, perhaps most appropriately read by a woman. The word 'perhaps' is an important one in this process. The technique is a simple one, requiring pupils to listen to what happens when a poem's reading is 'transmogrified'. What happens when Sylvia Plath's 'Daddy' is read by a male? What happens when one of John Donne's amorous poems – or his sermon on no man being an island – is read by a female? What happens when a Scots poem is read by an American, an Irish folk song by a West Indian, or this extract from John Agard's exuberant 'Poetry Jump-Up' by someone with an English voice and its distinctive cadence, pace and pronunciation?

> Words jumpin off de page
> tell me if Ah seein right
> words like birds
> jumpin out a cage
> take a look down de street
> words shakin dey waist
> words shakin dey bum
> words wit black skin
> words wit white skin
> words wit brown skin
> words wit no skin at all
> words huggin up words
> an sayin I want to be a poem today
> rhyme or no rhyme
> I is a poem today
> I mean to have a good time

Where a classroom is fortunate enough to have competence in two languages, colleges can work at translating a poem, to see if it can prosper in both. This is certainly a device which can be exploited in some parts of Canada. It can also be exploited elsewhere. What happens, for example, when colleges try to translate Andrew Salkey's droll 'Song for England' into English English?

> An a so de rain a-fall
> An a so de snow a-rain
>
> An a so de fog a-fall
> An a so de sun a-fail
>
> An a so de seasons mix
> An a so de bag-o-tricks
>
> But a so me understan
> De misery o de Englishman.

Again, this is a device for raising questions about poetry. How flexible can it be? How far can it tolerate other cultures, other tellings, other renderings? How universal is a poem? Dias's current work on cross-cultural responses to poetry suggests that poetry is a robust creature which can live and prosper across cultures. This particular exercise can help pupils explore this for themselves.

Language can be used, then, to explore poetry by playing games with it on one's own or in supportive communities. But it can also be used to comment on poetry. Nancy Martin (1976) has not been the only person to point out how important writing can be as a means of creating a discreet dialogue when a pupil does not wish to share views with others. A personal log can be a secret friend, a secret sharer, if someone decides to keep a commentary of some kind just for him or herself – someone to write down, to read, to think about. This again is a version of Josipovici's 'silence' and is to be respected, whether a pupil writes poetry within that privacy or writes about it. There may be a time when the teacher is invited in, to be a discreet and courteous guest. There may not. Either way, the teacher should accept as positive that such reflective engagement is going on.

There are individuals and, sometimes, colleges, who are prepared to be more public about their thoughts and feelings, and it is worth providing structures which they can choose from. One obvious device is to ask pupils to keep anthologies of poetry in which they interleave various components: poetry which they have read and liked; poetry of their own making; commentary on both. Such a collection serves two purposes, one short-term and one long-term. The short-term is fairly obvious: younger pupils often need concrete evidence of having achieved something and a fattening folder can provide it. That seems a fairly basic, practical view of how young minds work, but the process can be extended from this. If pupils are asked to keep an honest commentary on how they are getting on with poetry – how they fared with a poem they tackled on their own or in their college, or how they prospered in creating a poem of their own or in contributing to a collegial poem, such as a ballad – they are building a complementary, interwoven dossier to do with response.

It is this element which is worth developing. 'Writing logs' have been around for some time, with their invitation for pupil and teacher to see themselves as colleagues, chatting to one another on the page, confessing to problems, celebrating successes and providing one another with insights and advice on writing. The same can certainly happen with a poetry log, if the teacher signals that it really is a genuinely open-ended, unassessed opportunity for both partners to be honest and supportive in 'chatting' about what is going on in their writing and reading of poetry. Some teachers have experimented with cassette tapes instead, finding them more natural and akin to the gossip that Ingham espoused, and they are certainly worth trying. Either method involves a lot of work, as most worthwhile approaches do. Some pupils write little and may need to be approached through tutorial instead. Some write a great deal and need to be tactfully controlled. In either case, the teacher has to be a supportive, sympathetic but shrewd 'wise adult'. It is unrealistic to expect anyone to carry out such a scheme with every class all of the time. It has more chance of success when it is run with as many pupils as a teacher can honestly manage.

There is an alternative tactic. Often, such logs are used to create a dialogue between teacher and pupil, but they can also be used in the long-term to create an auto–dialogue – the pupil using his/her dossier in order to explore what has been happening, where he/she has come from, how he/she has changed. It does not take much setting up to ask pupils every half-year to research themselves. They can look at the poems which they have read, whether assigned or of their own choosing; the poems they have made; their comments on the reading processes they have engaged in and their responses to them. On this basis, they can set out to describe what has happened to them over the six-month period, how they feel that they have changed or maybe even grown and suggest what might be further ways forward for them.

Teachers might need to provide a framework in the early days. One school sets the task up as an information retrieval exercise under such headings as:

What have I read?
What sorts of poems were these?
What did I like?
What didn't I like?
What sorts of writing did I do?
How did I get on? Problems? Achievements?
How have I developed?
What approaches would I like to use again?
What else can I suggest?

Many pupils prefer to handle this task on their own, with the teacher as the only audience, but it is interesting how often adolescents are quite happy to accept the invitation to produce their reports in first draft and then get together in small colleges to share information and views, pooling their replies and handing in a group report.

There is one further use of the anthology, with its concurrent poetry and comment. Over the years of school, properly cared for, it grows into a considerable volume. It can certainly be assembled as a high-school activity. One of the properties of much poetry is that it sets out to be mnemonic – it is brief, it uses memory-raising devices of rhyme and rhythm, it uses language strikingly. An anthology can be one further means of making sure that poetry is retained, remembered – is given a chance to echo in the reader-owner's mind. The British editor Kaye Webb once produced a delightful collection of poetry chosen by children called *I Like This Poem* (1979). There is no reason why pupils should not look back towards the end of a phase of schooling and select their own anthology along similar lines, as individuals or as colleges, for their own pleasure or as collections of resources for other pupils. Perhaps we do not use our pupils as anthologizers enough.

There are several devices for turning pupils round into being providers of poetry on the old premise that we have the strongest felt need to learn when we have to teach! All of them engage pupils in exploring poetry for themselves in order to help others explore it. The most dramatic, perhaps, is to commission pupils to work out how they are going to explain a poem to someone from outer space. How are they going to get him to see that this poem has rhyme and rhythm and get him to grasp how these are affecting the poem's impact? How are they going to get him to see that those run-on lines suggest an energy which will not behave and stay within each line? How are they going to explain that some of this poem means more than it actually states? And so on. Some teachers find that approach a bit gimmicky, but it is interesting and valuable to commission colleges to find poems for a 'resource pool' to be used by a younger class or a class of their own age, and to discuss what it is in the poems and in themselves that has caused them to choose them. If the colleges have had experience of a range of approaches to poetry – dramatizing poetry, storyboarding, writing pastiche and so on – it can be equally valuable to get them to suggest techniques which their clients might find useful. Throughout the process, with its focus on another audience, colleges are in fact exploring the poems and the challenges they contain in their own terms as well. Some teachers experiment with having colleges produce task suggestion cards for the client groups to work from, but others may wish to think of other ways of using the material and suggestions they provide.

There is one other device which is worth exploring with senior pupils. It has already been suggested that poetry is a robust creature which travels well across cultures and even across languages. Nevertheless, it has its problems as it travels across oceans. American children are unlikely to be aware of the place in which Wordsworth was so moved by those flowers. Certainly, some Inuit children coloured their daffodils blue. English children can have no idea of the vastness of Canada or the intensity of its winter. At its most simplistic, some American children assumed that the foe in William Blake's 'The Poison Tree' was fine at the end of the poem and getting a sun tan; while British children saw a line about 'zero weather' in a Canadian poem as being about the worst temperature imaginable. Here is an opportunity for collegial sharing across cultures, between schools, as groups identify a set of topics – being young, old-age, living in town, the seasons, and so on – and agree to find poems which capture something of each topic within their culture. For example, colleges may find two or three poems to exchange on spring. They find material which explains spring in other terms – geographical, meteorological, photographic; accounts from journals and newspapers; their own comments on the season. Poems, supporting material, comment on these particular poems and why they have been chosen are made into a pack, to be sent to the other school. There is probably room for one pack every term, or maybe even two. Pupils are seeking and receiving poetry in order to share it, linking it to their personal experience and the culture within which they live. They are teachers and learners at the same time. With proper organization and support by their teachers, such a scheme can last for a year and sometimes for longer.

It has been a key theme of this book that pupils engage most powerfully with poetry when they are encouraged to use approaches which enable and require them to be concurrent teachers and learners. One small teacher-enquiry team in Britain (the ELSID group) has set out to devise such a method for use with secondary school pupils. It started from the work of Blackie (1971) who found herself uneasy with the conventional lesson in which her pupils found themselves isolates encountering a poem as an unseen text in a sudden confrontation, rather than enjoying an invitation and challenge to read, explore and create.

Blackie felt that she was an involuntary tyrant, setting up an agenda on her terms while ignoring and being ignorant of what her pupils might think, feel and wish to discuss. Her solution was to arrange for them to meet a poem before the lesson in which it was to be discussed. It might be issued for a few minutes at the end of another lesson, rather like a film preview, with the instructions that pupils were to read it and think about it and then write down some items for discussion. It might be issued as part of a homework assignment, again with instructions to write down those few comments. One important point was that the pupils had already had some time to encounter the poem before they met it in the classroom. The second was that they were having to do some thinking and feeling about it and jot their ideas down – as questions.

Blackie's thinking was elegant. Being able to express themselves in questions meant that pupils' genuine questions were hidden among pseudo-questions and both were contained in the privacy of writing intended for the teacher only. There could be no embarrassment now, if a pupil asked the meaning of a word or a phrase. Secondly, whatever a pupil might know or feel also appeared as a question, an invitation to respond. They might range from a pupil liking and 'knowing the meaning' of a tricky image to disliking a poem intensely. 'Why do I like the way that "wandered lonely as a cloud" suggests being miserable and damp?' offers other pupils the chance to comment. 'Why do I think this is a lousy poem?' prevents the premature closure which negative responses to poetry often cause and can open up others' honest opinions of the poem.

Blackie took in the pupils' jottings and produced from these a set of lesson guidelines for herself which responded to the agenda of preoccupations, doubts and insights which they had displayed. Her pupils came to the lesson having made some initial contact with the poem. Blackie came to the poem having made some initial contact with their responses to it. They were likely to be less dumb towards the poem; she less blind to what they had to offer and to where she might be able to help.

The ELSID teacher enquiry team saw the value in this process but decided to investigate whether the stage at which the lesson's conduct was taken back into the hands of the teacher could be transferred to the pupils instead. Like Dias, they arrived at the importance of a clear ritual for the pupils to use and become confident in. Once pupils are secure in it, they tend to use it unselfconsciously, choosing it from their toolkit of approaches when they feel it is most appropriate.

In the first phase, each pupil is given some time to spend with the poem and to think about it. With senior forms, about 15 minutes seems a sensible amount in which to read, consider and jot down five items about the poem in question form – about overall response, whether negative or positive; about particular lines or images; about items of vocabulary or grammar which cause pleasure or confusion; about echoes the poem creates. The next task for the pupil is to consider those five questions and to underline the three which are considered to be the most important for further work on the poem.

Concurrent teaching and learning start on a small, fairly intimate scale with the second phase, where pupils work in pairs, discussing and, where appropriate, answering one another's questions before going on to sort out three questions which are to be used in the next phase. Sometimes, pairs blend items; sometimes new ones arise from their discussion. The agenda is starting to form as a result of what the pupils have to say to one another, as they find their voices about the poem and their way into and around its mazes. At the same time, the teacher has a chance to be a genuine peripatetic observer and consultant, with time and opportunity to see and hear how they approach a poem and to identify their strengths, weaknesses and overall styles. Quite often, pairs choose the same items to go forward; sometimes, they disagree strongly. In both instances, the teacher can help pupils to explore and see why they have made these choices.

In the third phase, pairs are paired into groups of four and repeat the process of discussing the three questions which each pair brings. Again, the group is expected to edit its questions and to provide the three which it believes are most likely to promote further exploration and understanding of the poem. It also has to star the one which it believes to be of greatest potential interest and use to the plenary meeting in phase four. All three phases are run under very slight time pressure. Groups also have to cope with the pressure of needing to select items for increasingly public discussion, but at the same time they are being supported through the increasing collegiality.

Finally, the class comes into plenary. Each group takes on the task of presenting its starred item for discussion by the rest of the class. Many groups retain the question format but it is interesting how many will now move into statement, a sign of their increasing confidence with what they have to say. The other groups are allowed one or two minutes in which to reflect and prepare their response, for the entire process is intended to provide experience of maturing beyond the immediate and impulsive. The teacher's role is to make sure that each group makes some response to the initiating group's comment and to promote inter-group discussion and learning rather than learning which has the teacher as focus and fountain. If another group has starred the same item, it moves on to the second of its three, with the teacher noting that it is clearly one of interest to a lot of pupils if it has survived this far and appealed to eight people. Throughout the process, the teacher has to keep a nicely judged balance between allowing enough time for reflection and discussion and a slight sense of pressure of time and focus. She/he also has to practise skills as the plenary's chairperson and, at least with younger pupils in the secondary school, act as its cartographer, creating a map of what the students have brought to the poem and of what they have found and generated there. She/he may well need to produce a 'temporary terminus' for younger classes of what seems to have been achieved – the insights, the areas of agreement, of dissension and possible further consideration.

It is only after this stage that the teacher may choose to bring in some of her/his views and some of the agenda that she/he might have chosen. The students have had time to establish their interpretations first and to occupy the middle ground. The teacher arrives as a latecomer with further 'possibilities' – which means that her/his views must also be expressed as questions or as exploratory, tentative probings, proffered not as some form of correction but as further topics for groups to think about before they make their views known.

The results of such a session are far less predictable than a lesson in which the teacher confers agenda and knowledge upon pupils. Instead, its ritual has enabled and required everyone to confer with others about responses to a poem. It is important to make clear to pupils that such exploration does not always result in discovery for them and that this is an experience that we also know well – that we wise adults do not always 'succeed' with poetry either. That seems an important point to make as we also show that this approach, like many others described here and elsewhere, has encouraged dwelling with a poem in a spirit of collaborative enquiry in which everyone has rights of interpretation and responsibilities for their own and others' growing understanding of themselves and the poems they have encountered. The game has not been about 'solving poems out there' but coming to terms with the experience which they create, shift, and from time to time enhance.

This chapter has set out examples of techniques through which teachers can help pupils accept responsibility for their encounters with poetry. Many of these approaches flourish best when pupils become purposive, mutually supportive groups – colleges – although many are flexible enough to allow for privacy as well. All have the common theme of asking teachers to encourage pupils to see poetry as invitation to question – questioning poems, questioning visiting poets, questioning one another, their teachers, themselves. That does not imply some negative insecurity but the sense of adventure to be found in questioning's origin in the Latin verb 'to seek' and in Sir Thomas Browne's triumphant 'We carry within us the wonders we seek without us.' Properly encountered, poetry may help many to find and go on finding the wisdom of that statement.

6 International perspectives on the teaching of poetry: views from Australia, Britain, Canada and the USA

The arguments that have been developed and the suggestions for practice that have been offered are largely in response to a concern about poetry teaching; a concern that is shared by a large number of teachers both in Britain and in Canada. That concern is not a matter of disconsolate helplessness about any neglect of poetry or poor teaching, but rather a matter of some frustration that we now know so much more about acts of reading and responding to literature, about how children learn and about contexts that support or inhibit language performance, and yet are not always able to move consistently and coherently into practice that takes account of such knowledge.

This book is an attempt at such coherence and consistency, to link more closely aims and teaching approaches, to acknowledge the real capabilities of children and adolescents and to reduce constraints that affect both poetry and them. It is at the most practical level a wish to allow pupils the ownership and sharing of their own reading of poetry, akin to the ownership they assert when they talk informally about a book they have read voluntarily or a film they have watched on television.

When we invited four teachers to contribute an account of the state of poetry teaching in their countries, we hoped to discover what the constituents of this rather reduced global village might hold in common about what is exciting and what is problematical in the teaching of poetry in their countries. Why these countries? We could have enlarged the constituency to include other English-speaking countries as well as non-English-speaking countries. Such an enterprise is needed and demands a book on its own. Because of limitations on space and the constraints of time, we have limited ourselves to reports from colleagues in Australia, Britain, Canada and the United States. Their accounts are personal and not meant to represent official national positions on the teaching of poetry. The contributors are in a position to know what has been and is happening in the field and we are grateful for their informative and useful accounts.

The contributors were also asked to provide a short list of resources – print, audio-visual, and human – that were available in their countries and should be known internationally. It was felt such listings will make available to a wider audience 'local' materials that deserve to be better known, encourage the reading of poetry across a variety of cultures represented among the different national groups, and provide ideas for local initiatives. Generally, we hope these listings will be one step towards an international collaboration among teachers of English and bring their classrooms together in international exchanges that are becoming increasingly feasible through facilities afforded and made economical by computer networking.

There are remarkably similar concerns and positive developments in all four countries. There is a general recognition that poetry remains unpopular with a large proportion of the secondary school population and that such a situation can be attributed in part to New Critical influences on the teaching of poetry, particularly where this has led to the assumption by the teacher of the role of guardian of the poem's 'true meaning'. Contributors at the same time are generally agreed that there have been several productive developments. Some of these are:

1 A growing emphasis on pupils' writing poetry;
2 Concerted efforts to shift poetry off its pedestal, to make poetry an easily accessible and readily available art form;
3 An increasing willingness on the part of teachers to assign responsibility to pupils for the meanings they make;
4 A stress on collaborative small group work in discussing poetry, in choosing and enacting poems;
5 A recognition that pupils are more likely to take to poetry if they spend more time with contemporary poetry; and
6 The co-opting of a variety of media and art forms in celebrating poetry.

There is one concern that is hinted at in some of the contributions and directly stated by Bryant: that despite these gains there lingers a reluctance to surrender full power to readers, a reluctance demonstrated by a tendency somehow to direct the responding process along lines consonant with how reasonably competent readers of literature are said to proceed. 'Stages' in the responding process, and 'taxonomies' of the elements of responding are fine in their place; that is, as means of describing what happens in the transactions between readers and literary texts. To translate these stages and taxonomies into classroom procedures that *direct* response, however benignly, is to exercise a measure of control that, garbed in the best of intentions, denies pupils their autonomy as readers. Readers should be allowed to stray, to fail, to discover by indirection, to exercise intuition, to sense, to feel, and draw on experience, in order to provide for a truly literary reading. Such advocacy is not irresponsible romanticism; rather it is a reminder that truly responsible reading of poetry begins in a reader's trusting his or her response and working from and often away from that response. Again, it is important that we remind ourselves from time to time of Langer's truly wise observation: 'the entire qualification one must have for understanding art is responsiveness' (1953, p. 396).

Chapter 1 spoke of a tendency among many teachers to regard new developments in teaching as faddish and temporary shifts that return inevitably to the 'centre', wherever that is. If there is one intention that has directed the writing of this book, it has been to demonstrate that the theory and practices that have been proposed for the teaching of poetry derive from confirmations that have emerged over some time in several different fields of inquiry. The recognitions we point to are implicit in much good teaching of poetry; they are consistent with understandings of how adolescents learn and function productively in classrooms. Above all, these convergences have an explanatory power: they account for past failures *and* successes; they alert us to new possibilities. They suggest directions for how we must continue to proceed and where we must be particularly observant and questing. The contributions to this final chapter are themselves evidence that the directions and changes plotted in this book have acquired a considerable degree of momentum in at least four countries.

Teaching poetry in Australia – Ken Watson*

Until recently, poetry teaching in my home State of New South Wales – and, I suspect, in Australia as a whole – has been characterized by a profound unease. Teachers have been uncertain, indeed downright uncomfortable, in poetry lessons. Their own undergraduate training has not only failed to make them confident readers of poetry themselves, but has, at least until the dethronement of the New Criticism (a very recent event in most Australian universities) made them feel that there is one right interpretation of a poem that they must pass on to their pupils. This has, at least until relatively recently, led to a kind of teaching that concentrates on traditional poems (for which a 'right' interpretation can readily be obtained from the critics), that stresses the formal features of poetry, and that gives little or no weight to pupils' opinions. The popular school anthologies have been those that provide questions and activities after each poem, as well as explanatory notes.

The one bright spot in this rather dismal picture has been, from the mid-1950s onwards, a growing emphasis on the writing of poetry. This

*Ken Watson is Senior Lecturer in Education at the University of Sydney, New South Wales, Australia.

movement was given added impetus in 1967 with the publication of *English through Poetry Writing* by Brian Powell, a Canadian who was working in Australia at the time. Much more recently, two further books have reminded teachers of the value of such work in their classrooms: *A Book to Write Poems By* (Harris and McFarlane, 1983), and *The Writing of Poetry* (Mallick, 1986).

What makes a good poetry teacher, anyway? In her study of poetry teaching in Years (grades) 8 and 10 in the State of Victoria, Travers found one classroom where every pupil liked poetry lessons. What made this teacher stand out from the other 21 teachers in the study was

> his passion for local poetry, his wide selection of poems from which individual pupils could choose, and the seriousness and respect with which he accepted his pupils' offerings, whether they were commenting on other poems or writing their own. The accepting atmosphere of this classroom was in direct contrast to two parallel classrooms at the same level where poetry was disliked by most pupils (Travers, 1984, pp. 379–80).

Interestingly (indeed, humiliatingly – at least for those involved in teaching English at tertiary level) this teacher was a scientist without any training in literature.

Travers' study was carried out in the late 1970s. Today, if my observations of classrooms are at all typical, there are many more such teachers to be found. (And let us acknowledge that there were always at least a few such teachers, and that many of us would not have become poetry readers ourselves but for their influence.) What has brought about the change?

In the first place, I think there is a much greater acceptance now that enjoyment must come first. If poetry does not give pleasure, then little else that is positive will follow. This does not mean, of course, that poetry lessons should not be challenging: pupils want to be challenged, want to use their brains for thinking (the brain's main function, after all), not simply for rote learning and regurgitation. Anyone who has watched pupils in small groups arguing over the right words to be placed in a poem which has been presented with half a dozen gaps in it, or listened to them discussing how to present to the class a dramatic reading which will bring out the poem's essential qualities, knows that.

Secondly, there has been a growing awareness of the fact that the discrete poetry lesson, cut off from all other aspects of English, is not always the best way of presenting poetry. There has been a much greater concern to provide appropriate contexts: to introduce a poem as (to borrow a phrase from the Dartmouth Seminar) 'another voice in the conversation' when some topic of concern is being discussed, or to draw the class's attention to poems which touch on issues also raised in the novel or play being studied. Poems about loneliness are easily linked with Scott O'Dell's *Island of the Blue*

Dolphins; Langston Hughes' poems about racial prejudice are fine companion pieces to William Armstrong's *Sounder* or Harper Lee's *To Kill a Mockingbird*.

Thirdly, building on the work of Douglas Barnes and Frankie Todd, several Australian teachers have demonstrated the enormous value of small group talk about poems. Small-scale studies by Ryan *et al.* (1982), and a somewhat larger study by Hammond (1981) point not only to the way in which, in the non-threatening situation of the peer group, children develop and gain confidence in their ability to make sense of poems, but, in the case of Hammond's research, suggest further that small groups without a teacher present are more effective than groups with a teacher. It seems that teachers have great difficulty in shedding an authoritative role, and that when the teacher is in the group the discussion often suffers because the pupils are constantly attempting to follow the teacher's lead.

Finally, the overthrow of New Critical approaches to literature by the reader-response school of criticism is having a growing impact on Australian classrooms. Now that they realize that a range of responses, rather than a single right response, is acceptable, teachers are losing some of their uncertainty about approaching new poetry. The rise of reader-response theory has thus led both to a greater use of modern poetry to which the pupils can more readily relate and to teachers using the fact that pupils' initial reactions, however unformed, however simplistic, are necessary foundations upon which later, more profound responses are built.

In Australian classrooms today one can find:

1 Children in groups deciding on the questions that they, not the teacher, want to ask about a particular poem;
2 Pupils making their own selections from a wide range of poetry collections;
3 Groups arguing about the most appropriate poem to be placed at the beginning of a particular novel or to serve as an epilogue to it;
4 Groups preparing readers' theatre presentations of poems;
5 Groups arranging a cut-up poem in what seems to be the best sequence;
6 Pupils writing their own poetry;
7 Children providing various kinds of visual representation for poems (e.g. collages); and
8 Classes discovering the pleasures of choral verse.

While the most popular poets with younger children hail from overseas – Michael Rosen, for example – there seems little doubt that Bruce Dawe is the Australian poet who speaks most directly to older pupils. His collection, *Sometimes Gladness* (1978), should be available to every senior school student.

References

Dawe, B. (1978). *Sometimes Gladness*. Melbourne: Longman Cheshire.

Hammond, M. J. (1981). *Poetry with Teacher and Without*. Unpublished M.Ed. thesis. Melbourne: University of Melbourne.

Harris, R. and McFarlane, P. (1983). *A Book to Write Poems By*. Adelaide: Australian Association for the Teaching of English. ISBN 0 909955 42 5.

Mallick, D. (1986). *The Writing of Poetry*. Melbourne: Nelson. ISBN 0 17 006752 1.

Powell, B. (1967). *English through Poetry Writing*. Sydney: Novak.

Ryan, T., Sherock, T. and Robinson, D. (1982). Poetry and small groups. *Developments in English Teaching*, Nos 1 and 2, pp. 16–20 and 2–22.

Travers, D. M. M. (1984). The poetry teacher: behaviour and attitudes. *Research in the Teaching of English*, **18** (4), December, 367–84.

Texts

Australia is fortunate in that as well as locally produced texts it has ready access to the best available on the British market. While my own preference is for anthologies which present the poems without any additional material that might direct pupils' responses, I recognize that there will always be a need for 'teaching' anthologies, particularly for beginning teachers. The best of these are from Britain: the Bentons' *Touchstones* series (Hodder and Stoughton) and their *Poetry Workshop* (1975). One such Australian collection – a leader in its field, since the first edition was published some 20 years ago – is N. Russell and H. Chatfield's *New Poetry Workshop* (Melbourne: Nelson, 1983, ISBN 0 17 006186 8 (M)).*

A recently published anthology for junior secondary classes is Brian Keyte and Richard Baines' *A Phantom Script* (Melbourne: Nelson, 1986, ISBN 0 17 0067742 (J, M)). It does contain questions and activities, but fortunately not of the comprehension kind.

I have co-edited two anthologies which provide a range of poetry, most of it not previously anthologized, without questions and notes: Stephanie Eagles and Ken Watson, *The Climb and the Dream* (Melbourne: Macmillan, 1978, ISBN 0 333 25151 2 (J)), and Paul Richardson and Ken Watson, *Blue Umbrellas* (Sydney: Cassell/Methuen, 1981, ISBN 0 7269 9285 2 (M/S). A separate booklet of notes for the teacher is available for this latter collection, which attempts to take account of Australia's multicultural society by bringing together poets from 24 different countries.

Denise Scott's *Poetry Is* . . . (Melbourne: Heinemann, 1981, ISBN 085859 247 9 (M)), is an attractive anthology for middle secondary. There are activities of a general nature at the end of each section.

Two good collections for senior pupils are Anne Gunter's *Poems on My Mind* (Melbourne: Longman, 1981, ISBN 0 582 66198 6 (S/able M)), and John and Dorothy Colmer's *Pattern and Voice* (Melbourne: Macmillan, 1981, ISBN 0 333 33705 0 (S)).

---

*Where the letters J, M or S appear beside an item, they indicate that it is recommended for use at the Junior, Middle or Senior School levels.

Two very useful collections of performance poetry are: Rory Harris, *Take a Chance* (Adelaide: Australian Association for the Teaching of English, 1981, ISBN 0 909955 36 0 (J/M)), and Rory Harris and Peter McFarlane, *A Book to Perform Poems By* (Adelaide: Australian Association for the Teaching of English, 1985, ISBN 0 909955 55 7 (J/M)).

Audio-visual resources

A few years ago the University of Queensland Press produced a series of books and records of Australian poetry, but these were not a commercial success and are no longer available. There is, however, a useful cassette of Bruce Dawe reading his poetry: *Bruce Dawe Reads His Poems* (Melbourne: Longman, n.d., ISBN 0582 66540 X).

Human resources

The South Australian poet Rory Harris often visits schools to give poetry readings. He can be contacted through the Australian Association for the Teaching of English. The Fellowship of Australian Writers can put schools in touch with other practising poets.

Other resources

Helen Morris's invaluable UK reference book, *Where's That Poem?* (Blackwell), now in its third edition, has inspired *Find That Poem!*, edited by Ken Watson and Wayne Sawyer (Sydney: St Clair, 1984. ISBN 0 949898 10 4), an index by topic to ten widely used Australian anthologies.

David Mallick and Gill Jenkins' *Poetry in the Classroom* (Sydney: St Clair, 1983, ISBN 0 949898 06 6), is a collection of articles on the teaching of poetry taken from Australian, UK and US journals.

Teaching poetry in Britain – Brian Hirst*

Poetry around us and within us

According to a recent report by Her Majesty's Inspectors, poetry is given scant attention in English secondary schools. They found that English teachers tend to feel uncomfortable about teaching poetry and on average spend only 5% of their time on it. Given the diverse demands made upon English in the curriculum, it could be argued that that is a reasonable allocation. Certainly, few people outside school spend anything like 5% of their time reading or writing poetry. Nevertheless, if this uneasiness does exist, I suspect it is because of a feeling that poetry is somehow 'above' us (like metaphysics or God) rather than something which can surround us and be within us, given appropriate circumstances. Traditional literary criti-

*Brian Hirst is Head of English at John Flamstead School, Derbyshire, England.

cism, taught badly, has tended to reinforce the notion of poetry as a mystery to which we must humbly submit ourselves or some kind of teleological essence that we can share but not question. Structuralist theory, too, when taught badly, can be equally misleading, with crude structuralism asserting that tracing a poem's structures is enough to 'understand' or 'explain' it. And as Patrick Dias has already suggested, Post-structuralist theories, at their worst, sound like someone arguing with himself on some very abstruse point.

It seems to me that if we want the teaching of poetry to succeed with secondary school pupils some knowledge of literary theories is helpful – but we need to adapt them pragmatically in the constantly slippery context of the classroom. My contribution to this chapter, therefore, deliberately focuses on describing particular lessons in particular classrooms, to see how far theory and practice can be brought together. Here is how one secondary school starts its intake year's encounter with poetry.

First years – a 70-minute lesson

As the 12-year-olds come into the classroom they are given two A4 size pamphlets. The one with the white cover has the title '100 POEMS BY 100 PUPILS – JOHN FLAMSTEAD SCHOOL' and the green one the same title with 'SECOND ANTHOLOGY' added. The teacher explains that all the poems have been written by past and present pupils and asks the pupils to read the collections to themselves. Within a few minutes comes the expected deep silence, lasting for 20 minutes and more, with faces showing anything from mild interest to rapt attention. Then pupils start to point out poems to one another. 'Is this your brother's?' 'That's a good one.' 'Listen to this one.' The teacher joins the conversation. 'Do you know any of these writers?' 'Which poem did you like most?' After reading a few – one short and funny, one long and serious, another one sad, he asks if anyone else wants to read out a poem. The rest of the lesson is taken up with poem after poem being read out loud. It is as the teacher has expected – a 'magic' lesson which he, colleagues and pupils always enjoy.

Sequels to 'the magic lesson' can last up to eight more lessons over the next three weeks. The second lesson provides pupils with books and time to relax and immerse themselves in poetry, as they browse yet again through their pamphlets and three 'proper' poetry books as well, first as individuals reading quietly and then moving once more into talking, sharing, comparing. From here, paths can diverge. Individuals or groups might spend several lessons making cassettes of their poetry readings, with or without music and sound effects. They might each copy out a favourite poem on to a card and illustrate it, with the cards being bound for display, for another first-year class to read and finally for lodging with other poetry stock. Reading is constantly partnered by open, exploratory discussion.

Invariably, the lessons come to include the pupils writing poems them-selves, for display or for yet another genuine anthology. Poetry has been experienced as being around and within, intensively and extensively, with barriers removed wherever they can possibly be taken away.

And what happens as pupils near the end of their compulsory secondary education at 16? How far can their engagements with poetry retain those features of relaxed concentration, of conversation with and about a poem?

Fifth years – a 70-minute lesson

The class is in the final stages of its public examination course. From the course outline given at the start of the year, it knows that this month's assignments are *Writing your own poems* for the Language element and *A personal selection of three to six poems with commentary* for Literature. They already know that today's session is for preparatory reading and they pick up poetry anthologies and pamphlets from the range the teacher has laid out on tables at the front of the room. Some have brought song lyrics, some books from the school library. The atmosphere is nothing like rapt silence – more a noisy workshop. Nathan complains that he can't write poems. Jayne is already sifting through her poetry jottings and checking in 'Touchstones' that the haiku syllable pattern really is 5, 7, 5. Good. 'The Moods of Night' works – 'The daylight has lapsed / Nocturnal owl is alert / His eyes are agog.' Robert is busy impressing Wayne who scans 'The Charge of the Light Brigade' as Robert recites it, word-perfect. 'God, you're a genius, Trebor!' 'I know', smirks Robert. The teacher interrupts, reminding the class that the session is committed to looking for ideas and perhaps inspiration for their own poems and for the literature assignment. He suggests they might choose a child's poem, a classic and a modern poem. There are some scattered ironical groans and grumblings, but the teacher insists on silence for the next half hour – and almost gets it. They spend the last 20 minutes reading aloud, the teacher leading with Mike Harding's 'The Bogeyman' which raises laughter and the class wanting to know why they didn't have the anthology in which it appears in the first year. Then he reads Tennyson's 'Ulysses', to be greeted by a silence which might mean anything. Pupils read on from there, mainly concentrating on a new anthology. The session ends with Robert reciting 'The Charge of the Light Brigade' and Jayne reading her 'Moods of the Night'. The teacher gets a headache recording the titles of all the poetry books that 30 young people borrow before they leave the classroom.

After some four weeks of reading and discussing poems, the assignments are handed in. Many are impressive and touching. Later, some of the poems pupils have written are chosen for the pamphlet *Fifth Form Poems 1984/5*. A set is added to the school's poetry stock and is used alongside other texts for the poetry writing assignment in the following year. The teacher talks of that 'magic' silence appearing yet again as a class reads the pamphlet. It includes Philip's poem, 'Outward Bound':

> Our hearts sing out with pride,
> Our eyes shine bright with wonder,
> Sudden stillness takes the crowd
> As the rocket roars its thunder.
>
> All hold their breath a second,
> A second aeons long,
> As the rocket flees its pad,
> Jets screaming their fiery song.
>
> A daytime star it races,
> A sliver of straining steel,
> The rocket charges skyward,
> With unalloyed zeal.
>
> Out ride the sons of Terra,
> Far drives the thundering jet,
> Up leaps the race of earthmen,
> Out, far, and onward yet.

Samantha writes in the following year her 'Mr. Politician':

> Positioned high to make him tall
> He stands with back against the wall
> His voice so strong to those so weak
> Obsequious that he should speak.
> The people clap submissive hands
> Hypnotised by his commands.
> His bondsmen watch, remote controlled,
> Minds paralysed to overload.
>
> Mr. Politician, our liberator,
> I see you as a cruel dictator
> High in status, high in things
> Yet higher still, who pulls your strings?

Philip's favourite poem was Tennyson's 'Ulysses'; Samantha's, John Betjeman's 'The Businessman'.

The Concise Oxford Dictionary defines 'rapt' as:

Snatched away bodily or carried away in spirit from earth, from life, from consciousness or from ordinary thoughts and perceptions; absorbed, enraptured, intent.

Literary theory, from traditionalist to deconstructionist, is deeply committed to poetry as 'raptness'. A traditionalist might claim that poetry, by virtue of its total, seamless form, has this power to snatch us away. A Structuralist or formalist will ask how the poetry does this and perhaps answer that it is through the 'defamiliarization' of language – ordinary language snatched out of ordinariness and deployed in an intense and heightened way in poetic form. A deconstructuralist might refer to poetic language as having a quality of 'differance' – an admixture of 'to differ' and 'to defer'. Poetry differs from ordinary language and yet belongs to it; in poetry, language itself is not deferred, but its daily ordinariness is.

Where do these poetry lessons stand in all this theory? The answer is partly to do with pragmatism, partly to do with raptness. The bald fact is that most secondary school pupils do not read much poetry outside the classroom; that means that it is crucial that in school they encounter a *range* and *quantity* of reading matter. It is absurd to expect raptness or erudition to come about from occasionally reading two or three poems and discussing them in depth. A poetry 'lesson' is an empty space to be filled with the poems around us. An important question for all interested in the teaching of poetry is not '*How much time* is spent on poetry?' but '*How many poems* are encountered?' with its linked question 'What poems?' Like a traditionalist, I believe that poetry can have the power to snatch us away, to absorb us. Like the great structuralist (and post-structuralist) critic Roland Barthes, I believe this powerful fascination is partly due to the fact that when we read or hear a poem we are, in a sense, looking within ourselves. In the highly pluralistic society which is Britain today, it would be a nonsense to suppose that all young 'beginning' poetry readers and writers will 'find themselves' through studying within a traditional canon. Many teachers' experience of working with poetry has shown that interest, enjoyment, enthusiasm and fascination can be engendered through a much more eclectic approach to what may be called a poem – and that these responses can be brought about as much by reading other children's poems as through reading the work of established poets.

When Philip and Samantha read poems by other pupils, other poets, they read something about themselves – and turned to writing poetry from this. They were linguistically able. Neil was not – and Neil could also be difficult – but his experience of reading poems around and within him helped him to discover the fascinating power of poetry to control time, that elusive substance, within a form:

Disaster

9.59 on Sunday
Someone is shot
10.00 on Sunday
Someone is stabbed
10.01 on Sunday
Someone is mugged
10.02 on Sunday
Someone has a heart attack

On Sunday
It was a disaster!

Other contributors to this chapter and other chapters of this book have dwelt on the topic of developing response to poetry. This brief discussion has focused on a prior issue. Something must come before development and remain alongside it, nurturing it – and that 'something' is the experience of wide reading and hearing of the poems within and around us – including those we write ourselves.

I began this brief paper with HMI's concern for the teaching of poetry in schools, but, in a sense, their publication is a mark of poetry's increasing health in Britain. Poetry and poets seem to be undergoing something of a revival. Publishers talk of four million pounds worth of poetry books published this year. During National Poetry Week, newspapers carry pictures of poets reading their work on a London railway station and there is general acclaim for poems published in the advertisement spaces on London's tube trains. National poetry competitions for adults and children attract tens of thousands of entries, and readings are held anywhere, from local libraries to village halls. Perhaps the climate is improving after all.

Resources

Ideally, every English classroom should have its own poetry shelves, but too many teachers in Britain are made nomads, teaching English in several rooms and, in at least one instance, in the school dining hall. The days of a narrow canon of texts are over in many schools, replaced by sets of anything from 5 to 30 copies of particular anthologies accompanied, in some instances, by sets of pupils' poetry. Many schools invest in a wider stock through the school library's holdings of individual poets. Some hold sub-stocks of work by individual poets in a classroom or as portable boxes. Some make use of cassettes, either professionally produced or made by the pupils themselves. The list of books which follows is not exhaustive but gives some idea of the poetry resources available to anyone teaching poetry in Britain today.

Anthologies

Benton, M. and Benton, P. (eds) (1969). *Touchstones 1–5*. London: Hodder and Stoughton   The poems are arranged in themes and the series is excellent for introducing pupils to various poetic forms. So is *Poetry Workshop*, by the same editors and publisher.

Boyle, B. (ed.) (1983). *What's in a Poem?* London: Collins Educational   Two books of thematically arranged poems for the early years of secondary school, with an occasional page called 'What's in this poem?' A lively collection, mixing poems by established poets with poems by pupils.

Brownjohn, S. and Brownjohn, A. (eds) (1986). *Meet and Write*. London: Hodder and Stoughton   An exceptional series intended for the first three years of the secondary school. All the poems are modern, with the poets writing briefly about themselves and how they came to write the poems in the anthology. A supportive, exciting book, introducing many new names and new poems.

Foster, J. (ed.) (1981). *A Third Poetry Book*. Oxford: Oxford University Press   The first of an excellent series of three books of mainly light, modern poetry. The lavish, beautiful, colourful illustrations undoubtedly account for their widespread popularity and make them ideal for engendering the 'raptness' I regard as essential.

Harrison, M. and Stuart-Clark, C. (eds) (1977). *The New Dragon Book of Verse*. Oxford: Oxford University Press   A fine collection of mainstream traditional and modern poetry to choose from for the 11–16 age range.

Heaney, S. and Hughes, T. (eds) (1982). *The Rattlebag*. London: Faber and Faber   An excellent, fat anthology for 14-year-olds to lose and find themselves in, to read out loud from, to draw from, to write their own poems – and for the teacher to do the same.

Jones, R. (ed.) (1986). *Living Together*. London: Heinemann Educational   A good collection of poems from many cultures. One of a movement in publishing to recognize our multicultural society.

Kitchen, D. (ed.) (1987). *Axed Between the Ears*. London: Heinemann Educational   A lively, quirky collection chosen to appeal to pupils who said they didn't like poems until they encountered these. An example of British publishers putting their faith in teachers as editors of school anthologies.

Mansfield, R. and Armstrong, I. (eds) (1964). *Every Man will Shout*. Oxford: Oxford University Press   A well established book which remains an effective mixture of modern and pupil poets. Pupils are always impressed with the pupil poems, which are marked with an asterisk (*).

Orme, D. (ed.) (1987). *The Windmill Book of Poems*. London: Heinemann Educational   A fine anthology of an unusual range of poetry, compiled by the founder of the Schools Poetry Association. The commentary on the poems is careful and sensitive and is ideal for helping older pupils explore the poems and themselves.

Rosen, M. and Jackson, D. (eds) (1984). *Speaking to You*. London: Macmillan Education   A superb collection of poems to be read out loud, in a wide range of British idioms and dialects.

Smyth, W. (ed.) (1971). *Poems of Spirit and Action*. (2nd edn.) London: Edward Arnold   A fine collection for exploring nonsense form, limerick or ballad with younger pupils. Many of its poems are ideal for reading aloud or even memorizing, including many old chestnuts.

Styles, M. (ed.) (1984). *I Like This Stuff*. Cambridge: Cambridge University Press   An eclectic, enthusiastic range of poems from many cultures arranged to create all sorts of comparisons and links. A fine introductory book, as is its companion *You'll Love This Stuff*.

Poetry records and cassettes

Details available from:

Argo Spoken Word Cassettes   Decca Classics, P.O. Box 2JH, 52–54 Maddox Street, London W1A 2JK.

Caedmon Spoken Word Series   Gower Publishing Co. Ltd., Gower House, Croft Road, Aldershot GU11 3HR.
Chivers Sound and Vision   93–100 Locksbrook Road, Bath BA1 3HB.

Teachers' books

Andrews, R. (1983). *Into Poetry – An Approach Through Reading and Writing*. London: Ward Lock Educational   An excellent practical book, made up of ten units of ideas for each year of the secondary school, all designed to develop awareness of how poetry achieves 'differance' through form.

Benton, P. (1986). *Pupil, Teacher, Poem*. London: Hodder and Stoughton   An exploration of teachers' attitudes on how to teach poetry, leading to discussion of further approaches, many of which chime with the views of this book.

Brownjohn, S. (1980). *Does it Have to Rhyme?*. London: Hodder and Stoughton   An excellent practical book on ways of promoting 'raptness' with poetry and its forms by writing it. Ideal for younger pupils, as is its companion *What Rhymes with Secret?* (1982).

Ede, J. and Calthrop, K. (eds) (1984). *Not Daffodils Again – Teaching Poetry 9–13*. London: Longman (Schools Council)   After the sardonic title, a lot of 'spin-off' suggestions about working with poetry and younger pupils.

Hughes, T. (1979). *Poetry in the Making*. London: Faber and Faber   A book by a major poet including his famous description of how his poem 'The Thought-Fox' arrived. A book for older pupils to read or for the teacher to quote from with younger classes.

Stibbs, A. and Newbold, A. (1983). *Exploring Texts Through Reading Aloud and Dramatisation*. London: Ward Lock Educational   A useful book for teachers wanting to extend engagement with a text beyond talking and writing about it.

Tunnicliffe, S. (1985). *Poetry Experience*. London: Methuen   After arguing for the importance of poetry, the author presents many practical suggestions for the classroom and provides several lists of information.

And three books on current literary theory:

Corcoran, W. and Evans, E. (eds) (1987). *Readers, Texts, Teachers*. Milton Keynes: Open University Press   A book for those who wish to look more fully at current ideas on reader-response theory from Britain and Australia.

Eagleton, T. (1983). *Literary Theory*. Oxford: Blackwell   A comprehensive, committed and entertaining account of a complex subject.

Griffith, P. (1987). *Literary Theory and English Teaching*. Milton Keynes: Open University Press   A highly readable survey of what has happened in response theory over recent years, linked to some practical suggestions for the classroom – and the occasional quietly worded challenge, perhaps.

Journals

There are three nationally available journals (three issues a year) for teachers of English in Britain, and all give extensive coverage to teaching poetry. The first two are particularly useful for teachers working in culturally pluralistic schools.

English in Education (Journal of the National Association for the Teaching of English)   NATE Office, 49 Broomgrove Road, Sheffield S10 2NA. Members of NATE also receive *The English Magazine* and belong to a discount scheme for the ILEA English Centre's publications.

The English Magazine (Journal of the Inner London Education Authority English Centre)   The English Centre, Sutherland Street, London SW1.

The Use of English   Scottish Academic Press (Ref U/E), 33 Montgomery Street, Edinburgh EH7 5JX.

And there is also *Poetry Review*, a good way of keeping in touch with what is happening in poetry. Each issue contains reviews and poems. Poetry Review, Subscription Department, 21 Earls Court Square, London SW5 9DE.

Further resources

This list suggests starting with local expertise, working outwards to nationally available resources.

Local Education Authority English Advisers can often help cut the cost of the richest of all resources, a live poet, by arranging for the poet to visit a group of schools. Sometimes, they have access to funds to help pay the poet's fees. They also keep detailed information on local and national events to do with poetry and are often happy to get involved with local events themselves.

The local library is an invaluable source for details of local poetry events. Most are happy to inform teachers of recent acquisitions and will accept poetry displays from their local schools.

Regional Arts Associations have lists of poets who are willing to work in schools and have details of how they can help finance visits by poets. You should be able to obtain the address of your region's Arts Association from the local library or English Adviser, or from *The Arts Council of Great Britain*, 105 Piccadilly, London W1V OAU.

The Poetry Society now has its own Education Department at 21 Earls Court Square, London SW5 9DE, which deals with poetry courses, poetry competitions and events and with its own 'Poets in Schools' Scheme.

The Schools Poetry Association is run by teachers for teachers. Its *Schools Poetry Review* enables everyone interested to share ideas. Contact SPA at Twyford School, Winchester SO21 1NW for information about its publications and activities.

Teaching poetry in Canada – Coralie Bryant*

The teaching of poetry in secondary classrooms across Canada is changing. The evidence is not yet overwhelming, but the signs are of a transition taking place from a New Critical to a response-centred approach to the

---

*Coralie Bryant is Consultant, Secondary Language Arts at Winnipeg School Division No. 1, Winnipeg, Manitoba, Canada.

teaching of literature – and this has particularly affected the teaching of poetry.

There are a number of reasons for this. A higher percentage of our students stay on through high-school than did, say, 20 years ago; the social composition and ability range of the student population has changed dramatically, and conventional approaches do not meet students' needs the way they once seemed to. Secondly, research in the learning of language, and the growth of both Reader-response Theory and the Response to Literature movement have had a profound impact on the development of curricula. Nearly every Canadian province has produced a response-centred curriculum within the last decade. As they are implemented, these curricula serve as catalysts, helping teachers in the difficult job of shaking traditional practice.

In Canada, education is a provincial affair; that is, all matters regarding curriculum and schools are supervised by departments of education under provincial jurisdiction. Despite this decentralized system, there presently exists a remarkable unanimity among provincial documents. This is largely due to the influence of the Canadian Council of Teachers of English. Through its annual conference – an arena of interaction among British, Australian, American and Canadian educators – and the two professional journals, *English Quarterly* and *The Canadian Journal of English Language Education*, CCTE has developed a fairly cohesive professional community.

In many ways, Canada's geographical location and its historical affiliations have been entirely advantageous for the teaching of English. English teaching in Canada has felt the influences of developments from both Britain and the United States, often providing fertile ground for the exchange of ideas from both sides of the Atlantic – and more recently from Australia as well. International conferences are examples of such cross-fertilization: the First International Conference on Writing was held in 1979 at Carleton University in Ottawa under the auspices of the CCTE, and in 1986 the Fourth International Conference of the International Federation of Teachers of English was also held in Ottawa. If curriculum documents across Canada seem remarkably current in the principles and practices they advocate, this may partly be due to those international visitors who have stayed on to engage curriculum designers and work with English teachers in Canada.

When one examines these documents, it is clear that one of the more powerful influences on approaches to the teaching of literature is the work of Rosenblatt, particularly as it is represented in her influential book, *The Reader, the Text, the Poem: The Transactional Theory of the Literary Work* (1978). An important Canadian influence has been the work of Reading theoretician, Frank Smith, who has argued for the active role of readers in the creation of meaning. As these new curricula are implemented, teachers and English consultants across the country report that teachers are gradually moving away from the traditional intensive analysis of a very few poems from an established canon, and moving towards developing response to a much wider range of poetic forms.

The appearance of new 'integrated' textbooks, with literature organized thematically, makes this job easier in some ways, suggesting that literature might be approached through ideas, through meaning, and not mainly through form or graphic representation. Fillion and Henderson's *Inquiry into Literature* (Collier Macmillan 1980), the first integrated series based on the response model has done much to influence teachers toward an inquiry approach. *Contexts* (Nelson) for grades 7–10 or *Connections* (Gage) for senior high-school pupils are more recent examples of such texts. For the teaching of poetry these texts do not entirely satisfy, for while they encourage a way in through ideas and experience, they do not provide enough poems to encourage comparison of structure and form within the genre. Nevertheless, the movement toward integrating the language arts has done much to bring more poetry teaching into the schools.

Some teachers have observed that there is so much more writing of poetry in secondary classrooms and that, because of this, students are more open to reading and studying poems. A dramatic increase in the amount of expressive writing has particularly influenced the trend toward the writing of poetry. One Ontario high-school teacher reports that by the time students reach grade 10, they have been writing in journals for years and show little resistance to writing of all kinds: rather than producing a mere 'spontaneous overflow', students work with relative ease toward shaping the results into more public forms. Poetry, whose forms have opened up so much in this century, grows easily out of the expressive mode, easing the job for teachers introducing poems for study. Brian Powell's *Making Poetry* (1971) has been enormously helpful to Canadian teachers as they encourage students to write poems. Teachers like Pat Lashmar (*Poetry in Focus*, 1983) have joined Powell in giving workshops for teachers in poetry writing, as have professional writers through the sponsorship of the League of Canadian Poets. The various provincial arts councils sponsor the presence of poets in the schools, programmes which have done much to promote the importance of the genre.

It appears that the emphasis on process in writing (and reading) may be having an additional impact on the teaching of literature. In the best teaching, a shift has occurred from using a model in which the teacher reads and presents an interpretation to one of developing sensitive, intelligent readers who know how to slow down their own reading of a text. As with writing, teachers are learning to intervene, and teach students strategies for intervention, in the process of reading and developing response. Russell Hunt of St. Thomas' University, New Brunswick ('Toward a process intervention model in Literature teaching', *College English*, 44, 1982, 345–57) describes several such interventions to help students effectively slow down their readings so that they can experience and value it.

Small-group work is rapidly becoming the most common method of helping students to become engaged owners of the text before they are expected to interpret or evaluate it. For example, small groups develop and perform a reading of a poem; various renderings of the poem are then discussed. The cloze technique is used either in small-group or whole-class settings: certain words are 'whited out' and students collaborate to complete the poem. The result is close attention to language as they grapple with the poem's sense. Students are sometimes asked to develop questions for the poet, or to order stanzas which have been cut apart. All these collaborative strategies, and others, invite discussion of meaning without first shaping it according to the teacher's interpretation. Students participate actively, using their own language to construct meaning as they read and talk about the text.

Patrick Dias of McGill University has developed a collaborative model to encourage independent readers of poetry, which eliminates initial shaping by the teacher in the form of questioning or directions and encourages full responsibility on the part of students for the meanings they make. The Quebec curriculum incorporates the model within its literature section. Teacher Rudi Engbrecht from Winnipeg (see 'Individualizing Approaches to Poetry' in S. Tchudi's (ed) *English Teachers at Work*, Boynton-Cook 1986) uses it extensively to develop student autonomy in the reading of all kinds of literary texts. Teachers in many locations are trying this collaborative model to help them in two particularly troublesome areas: the teaching of poetry, and the effective use of small groups as a dominant mode of instruction. Others have responded to this research by introducing a literary journal for students to work out their responses to literature as they read and discuss it.

Somewhere between the highly structured literary critical approach – still the rule, perhaps, rather than the exception in Canadian classrooms – and the student-centred model, is the position that students need to be taught the 'stages' or 'levels' of response. The Alberta Curriculum presents the elaboration of personal response as happening through three stages: finding the literal meaning, interpretation and evaluation. These categories are reminiscent of Purves' (1968) elements of response: engagement, perception, interpretation and evaluation.

Such distinctions unquestionably help teachers to understand the process and to sequence activities around texts. The question is whether those levels should be presented as a heuristic to students. The authors of one new high-school poetry text based on the response model seem to take that position; Glen Kirkland and Richard Davies in a chapter of *Inside Poetry* called 'Becoming Critical Readers', present the student with four 'levels of response': *engagement*, *understanding content* ('clarifying the unknown' and 'understanding purpose'), *form develops content*, and *evaluation*. Although it could be argued that these stages roughly parallel what actually happens to students using the Dias model, the question is whether students' capacity to become mature readers of poetry is helped or hindered by conscious application of such stages.

It comes down, perhaps, to the question of autonomy. Do we, as Bryant Fillion suggests, teach students *how* to 'interrogate the text' or do we first stand aside as they ask their own questions? Do we let their choral readings and oral interpretations shape the discussion of meaning or do we teach them a heuristic to help lead them through their readings of a text? There is a danger, as there has been with teaching writing as process, of reifying a multi-levelled response model. Perhaps, given our students' characteristic distaste for poetry, teachers might view with caution those developments that 'manage' reading and 'stage' responses.

Selected texts

Atwood, M. (1982). *The New Oxford Book of Canadian Verse in English*. Oxford: Oxford University Press. ISBN 0 19 540396 7 (S)   Beginning with Robert Hayman in the sixteenth century, this volume includes two or three poems by a great many Canadian poets in chronological order. Particularly strong on recent, and female, poets, and valuable for Atwood's introduction.

Cameron, B., Hogan, M. and Lashmar, P. (1983). *Poetry in Focus*. Globe/Modern. ISBN 0 88996 066 6 (M, S)   Loosely organized under 'kind' of poems – narrative, lyric, ballads, and free forms but organized again under those titles either by form or by theme. Strength: the large number of poems, chosen clearly with the interests of adolescent students in mind.

Cooley, D. (1981). *Draft: An Anthology of Prairie Poetry*. Winnipeg: Turnstone Press. ISBN 0 88801 037 0 (S)   A comprehensive collection of the new poetry written by poets from the prairie, or poems about the prairie. In all there are 61 poets, including Eli Mandel, Robert Kroetsch, David Arnason, Andrew Suknaski, Pat Lane, Lorne Crozier and W. D. Valgardson.

Downie, M. A. and Robertson, B. (1984). *The New Wind has Wings: Poems from Canada*. Oxford: Oxford University Press. ISBN 0 19 540431 9 (bound) (J, M)   Spans the entire history of Canadian poetry, presenting dozens of poems in a beautifully illustrated volume. Also available in paperback.

Geddes, G. and Bruce, P. (1978). *15 Canadian Poets Plus 5*. Oxford: Oxford University Press. ISBN 0 19 540289 8 (S)   The intent of this volume is to provide a selection of the best post-war Canadian poetry in English. The strength of the text is that it provides enough poems by each author to give a real sense of that poet's range and contribution.

Glassco, J. (1970). *The Poetry of French Canada in Translation*. Oxford: Oxford University Press. ISBN 0 19 540167 0.

Hatt, B. E. (1983). *Easterly: 60 Atlantic Writers*. Toronto and London: Academic Press. ISBN 0 7747 1219 8 (S)   Focused on the work of more recent writers, including Hugh MacLennan, Harold Horwood, Alistair MacLeod, Alden Nowlan, E. J. Pratt, and many younger poets.

Head, J., Laing, D. and Miller, G. (1976). *Signatures: Poems of Canada*. Windsor: Nelson. ISBN 0 176 00418 1 (M, S)   In three volumes, this series makes available a wide range of more recent Canadian poems in an attractive format. Delightful poems to use with students.

Kirkland, G. and Davies, R. (1984). *Inside Poetry*. Toronto and London: Academic Press. ISBN 0 7747 1224 4 (S)   Material predominantly Canadian, with a fair number of American and British poems, intelligently chosen for the late junior high or senior high student. Chapter 1 is 'an introductory immersion', with no exercises, Chapters 2–7 are an introduction to the study of poetry with poems, prose and exercises, while Chapter 8 contains over 100 poems grouped according to theme, with exercises. Very helpful. Appendices as well. Teacher's Guide comes in a huge binder.

Nowlan, M. (1983). *Stubborn Strength*. Toronto and London: Academic Press. ISBN 0 7747 1214 7 (S)   Subtitled 'A New Brunswick Anthology', this volume collects poetry written in the province since the 1790s, grouping them by period.

Weaver, R. and Toye, W. (eds) (1981). *The Oxford Anthology of Canadian Literature*, 2nd edn. Oxford: Oxford University Press. ISBN 0 19 540376 2 (S)   A collection of Canadian writing from the 1700s to the early 1980s, arranged alphabetically by authors' names (the text does, however, provide lists of themes, subjects, periods and regions). Rather extensive biographies introduce each author's work.

Woolatt, R. and Souster, R. (1980). *Poems of a Snow-eyed Country*. Toronto and London: Academic Press. ISBN 0 7747 1124 8 (S)   Organized by region. Begins with six verse statements about what it means to be Canadian, then presents poems from the Atlantic, Quebec, central Canada, the prairies, the West Coast, and the Yukon. Thematic groupings also provided.

For ideas in teaching the writing of poems

Powell, B. (1973). *Making Poetry*. London: Collier Macmillan. ISBN 02 973440 1 (J, M, S).

Films

Films on Canadian Poetry   A series of seven short films based on poems by: M. Atwood, E. Birney, I. Layton, A. Nowlan, A. Purdy, F. R. Scott and R. Souster. Available from Marvin Melnyk Associates, Ltd, Box 220, Queenston, Ontario LOS 1Lo.

Poets on Film – 1 (National Film Board of Canada (NFB), 8 min. colour)   Interpretations of 'Riverdale Lion' by J. R. Colombo, 'A Kite is a Victim' by L. Cohen, 'Klaxon' by J. Reaney and 'The Bulge' by G. Johnston.

Poets on Film – 2 (NFB, 8 min., colour)   Interpretations of 'Hazel Bough' by E. Birney, 'Travellers Palm' by P. K. Page, 'Death by Streetcar' by R. Souster and 'A Said Poem' by J. R. Colombo.

Poets on Film – 3 (NFB, 7 min., colour)   Interpretations of 'Perishing Bird' by D. G. Jones and 'Mon Ecole' by S. Garneau.

Wood Mountain Poems (NFB, 28 min., colour)   Describes the Wood Mountain area of Saskatchewan where Andrew Suknaski has produced his poems.

Progressive Insanities of a Pioneer (CAN, 15 min., colour)   Margaret Atwood reads her poem of the same name.

Alden Nowlan (NFB).

Margaret Atwood (NFB).

Milton Acorn (NFB).

Aloud/Bagatelle (NFB, 6 min.)   Performance of Birney's sound poem about trains, 'To Swindon from London by Britrail'.

Earl Birney: Portrait of a Poet (NFB, 53 min.).

A. M. Klein: The Poet as Landscape (NFB, 58 min.).

Autobiographical by A. M. Klein (NFB, 10 min.)   Focus on Klein's perceptions of Montreal.

Dorothy Livesay: The Woman I Am (NFB, 40 min.).

F. R. Scott: Rhyme or Reason (NFB. 57 min.).

Morning on the Lievre (NFB, 13 min.)   Portrays the Lievre River in autumn accompanied by reading of Lampman's poem.

Poen (NFB, 4 min.)   Leonard Cohen reads his prose poem from *Beautiful Losers*.

Poetry readings on tape

Canadian Poets on Tape. This series contains readings by E. Birney, I. Layton, F. R. Scott, R. Souster, G. McEwen, D. Livesay, A. Purdy, J. Reaney and M. Waddington. Available from Van Nostrand Reinhold Ltd., 1410 Birchmount Road, Scarborough, Ontario M1P 2E7.

Modern Canadian Poets: A Recorded Archive features Birney, Brewster, Cogswell, Johnston, Layton, Livesay, Marriott, Page, Purdy, Scott, Smith, Souster and Waddington. League of Canadian Poets.

CBC Learning Systems: has a catalogue listing its complete audiotape holdings. Contact: CBC Enterprises, P.O. Box 500, Station A, Toronto, M5W 1E6.

Records

Alden Nowlan's Maritimes (CBC Learning Systems T-57193-4).

The Poetry and Voice of Margaret Atwood (Caedmon C 1537).

The Twist of Feeling (on Atwood) (CBC Learning Systems).

Canadian Poets 1 (CBC Publications). Birney, Bowering, Cohen, Layton, MacEwen, Newlove, Purdy.

Layton Reads His Own (Caedmon ML 70002).

6 Montreal Poets (Folkways 9805).

6 Toronto Poets (Folkways 9806).

Other resources

Poets Frank Davey and Fred Wah launched the world's first national electronic magazine two years ago in Toronto, with poetry as its focus. *Swiftcurrent* concentrates mainly on poetry, and is housed in a VAX 750 at York University in

Downsview, Ontario, accessible from Datapac and telephone to readers with modem-equipped microcomputers anywhere in Canada. For subscriptions and further information, write to: Swiftcurrent, 104 Lyndhurst Avenue, Toronto, Ontario M5R 2Z7.

Most provinces have an Arts Council which in some cases has a programme to subsidize readings or school workshops. In Manitoba, for example, the Manitoba Arts Council sponsors the Artists in the Schools Programme which puts schools in touch with Manitoba artists of all kinds, and subsidizes the cost of their working in classrooms. For information on funding readings by Canadian poets, write to: Canadian Council for Public Readings by Canadian Writers, Writers and Publications Section, The Canada Council, 255 Albert Street, Box 1047, Ottawa, Ontario K1P 5V8, or call 1-800-267-8282 (toll-free).

The League of Canadian Poets and Writers Union of Canada sponsor workshops and readings. For more information, write to or call: The League of Canadian Poets, 24 Ryerson Avenue, Toronto M5T 2P3 – (416) 363-5047, or Writers Union of Canada, 24 Ryerson, Toronto M5T 2P3 – (416) 868-6914 or the provincial writers' guild or union (e.g. Manitoba Writers' Guild) or the branch of the Canadian Authors Association found in each major city. The Toronto branch: same address as above, phone (416) 364-4203.

Teaching poetry in the United States – Susan Tchudi*

The teaching of poetry in secondary schools in the United States is a 'hodge podge' of approaches and activities that represent very diverse theories of what poetry is. For some, poetry is an intuitive experience in which the affective response of the reader is central. For others, poetry reading is an intellectual activity that requires the reader to engage in analysis in order to uncover meaning. For some, poetry reading is an activity that one does; for others, it is an experience which one has.

One thing that seems clear to teachers in the US is that students hate poetry. At presentations at national conferences and in articles in journals, teachers begin their discussions about how to teach poetry with the admission that the unit will be greeted by groans and objections from students. And teachers of very differing approaches all purport to have found a way to make poetry, in the words of one teacher, 'ouchless' (Don Mainprize, 'Ouchless poetry', *English Journal*, February 1986, 31–3).

Teachers' theories about what poetry is for, of course, determine the approaches they take in teaching it. For the most part, teachers are concerned about poetry that speaks to the lives of the students. Although some teachers report success in teaching poetry of other eras ('What's an old poem [pre-1900] that works with kids?', *English Journal*, November 1983, 73–9), many recommend that teachers eschew the use of the traditional

*Susan Tchudi works in the Department of English Language and Literature, Central Michigan University, Mount Pleasant, Michigan.

anthology which contains a chronological representation of classic poems, and look in trade anthologies for poems selected specifically for young people. They also recommend that teachers begin with humour, use rock music lyrics, browse through varieties of poetry collections, and allow students to do the same, making their own selections for the poetry that will be considered in class.

Although all teachers are concerned that students learn to understand and appreciate poetry, their methods for achieving that goal are very diverse and sometimes conflicting. Teachers who boldly state that it is their role to point out the difference between good poetry and mediocre poetry are not common (although such teachers do exist). In fact, most teachers recognize that it is the mystification of poetry through the use of jargon and teacher explication of secrets of poetic meaning that have created the antipathy that students have for poetry, and most want to help students learn to understand poetry on their own. Despite a growing awareness that technical terminology often throws up roadblocks for students, it is still the most common way students are taught how poetry means. Some teachers begin with a simplified list of 'the poet's tools' believing that knowing how a poet uses these tools will help the student both understand the poem and appreciate it.

Some teachers have found that they are able to help students get to the meaning of a poem without introducing technical terminology but by focusing on the elements of the poem that they see as central to helping students understand meaning. Often, then, with this approach the teacher is still very much in control. Although the meaning is arrived at in a dialogue between the teacher and students, the questions are the teacher's: 'Why does the poet use this particular word?', 'What does the title mean?', 'How does the rhythm affect the tone?' and so forth. Teachers using this technique also find that they can teach technical terminology in the process of discussion and in a way that is more meaningful than using poetry as illustrative of lists of poetic devices.

Music, dance, art and drama are other means that teachers have used to help students discover/uncover/create the meaning of a poem. For some teachers, combining poetry with other artistic media is a means of getting at common technical elements, for example, the rhythms involved in music, dance and poetry; or the use of imagery in both poetry and graphic arts. Drama is often used as an activity for students to demonstrate that they understand the meaning of the poem rather than as a means of coming to an understanding; that is, students are asked to represent the meaning by recreating the poem or the theme of the poem in a dramatic situation. Sometimes art and music are used to provide a setting for the poem.

Writing has been used in a number of ways as a means to understand poetry. A common use is for students to write poetry so that they can understand the process and the techniques that poets use. Sometimes this means teaching poetic techniques *a priori* and having pupils use these in their own efforts; sometimes teachers provide formulas for students to follow; sometimes students are given model poems as 'inspiration' for their own work. Better practices combine the reading and writing of poetry and provide students with a more open-ended and fluid relationship between what they read and what they write. Writing has also been used as a means of understanding a specific poem rather than understanding how poetry works. One such practice grows out of the transactional theories of literature of Rosenblatt, Holland and Bleich. Based on the notion that students create meaning on the basis of their background knowledge and experience, some teachers have had students record in writing their reactions to poetry as they read it.

The practice of having students come to the meaning of a poem on their own is not as common as formalistic approaches to teaching poetry, but it is one that shows promise because of its consistency with current theories of reading and writing processes. Some teachers have demonstrated their belief in the value of students determining what is meaningful to them by having them select and collect literature that they like for consideration in class or for inclusion in their own anthologies. Some teachers have taken this a step further by assigning students in small groups the task of making meaning of a poem as a problem-solving activity.

Recent researchers in this area are looking in more detail at the process that students engage in as they encounter a poem and make meaning of it. In the US the work of Robert Blake and Anna Lunn on poetry protocol analysis concludes: 1. The process of reading a poem is not a simple, easy, linear, instantaneous task. 2. Few students are aware of the processes available to them for a satisfactory reading of a poem. 3. Individuals respond differently to the same poem. 4. Within the limits of the agreed upon meaning held by a class of students and by the larger community there are as many responses to a complex and sophisticated poem as there are students in a class ('Responding to poetry: high school students read poetry', *English Journal*, February 1986, 68–73).

Although the US market is dominated by textbooks that take a formalistic approach to poetry, there is a growing interest in and knowledge about transactional theories of literature. Teachers are willing to be convinced that students 'with no prior instruction in the apparatus of literary criticism, with no knowledge of special terms for figurative language or the technical aspects of poetry – [are] able to "work through" and "understand" a poem in a way that is eminently satisfying' (ibid., p. 73).

Anthologies

Dunning, S., Lueders, E. and Smith, H. (eds) (1967). *Reflections on a Gift of Watermelon Pickle . . . and other Modern Verse*. New York: Lothrop, Lee and

Shepard. ISBN 0 688 51231 3 (M, S)   This book of 114 poems has remained popular for 20 years because of its wide range of poems that are about real life – from arithmetic and animals to music and food. Illustrated with black and white photos.

Dunning, S., Lueders, E. and Smith, H. (eds) (1969). *Some Haystacks Don't Even Have Needles and Other Complete Modern Poems*. New York: Lothrop, Lee and Shepard. ISBN 0 688 414451 (M, S)   An equally popular sequel to *Reflections on a Gift of Watermelon Pickle*. Illustrated with colour art reproductions.

Hopkins, L. B. (1980). *Morning Noon and Nighttime, Too* (compilation). New York: Harper and Row. ISBN 0 06 002576 9 (J)   A slim volume of 42 poems for young readers that describe the activities that one experiences in the day from getting up to going to bed. Illustrated by Nancy Hannan.

Janeczko, P. (ed.) (1977). *The Crystal Image*. New York: Dell Publishing Co. ISBN 0 440 91553 8 (S)   Nine thematic units: The World Around Us, Sports, Places/Things, Glad Love, Sad Love, Aloneness, Young People, Past Youth, Death. The poets are primarily contemporary but the collection includes some nineteenth century poets too.

Janeczko, P. (ed.) (1981). *Don't Forget to Fly: A Cycle of Modern Poems*. Scarsdale, N.Y.: Bradbury Press. ISBN 0 87888 187 5 (S)   Seventy modern poets including a good representation of women, such as Adrienne Rich, Marge Piercy and Joyce Carol Oates.

Janeczko, P. (1984). *Strings: A Gathering of Family Poems* (compilation). Scarsdale, N.Y.: Bradbury Press. ISBN 0 02 747790 8 (M, S)   Many lesser known poems are represented but the poems are wonderful: funny, joyful, sad, touching and filled with warmth.

Koch, K. and Farrell, K. (1981). *Sleeping on the Wing: An Anthology of Modern Poetry with Essays on Reading and Writing*. New York: Random House. ISBN 0 394 50974 9 (S)   This collection includes a number of poems by each of 23 modern poets starting with Walt Whitman. The essays provide entries into the poems showing how they become accessible and discuss writing poetry related to what one has read.

Larrick, N. (ed.) (1977). *Crazy to Be Alive in Such a Strange World: Poems about People*. New York: M. Evans and Co. ISBN 0 87131 225 5 (M)   Nine selections devoted to people by poets who write for children – Shel Silverstein and Eve Merriam to grown-up's poets – Nikki Giovanni, Tennessee Williams, Galway Kinnell. Photographs by Alexander L. Crosby.

Livingston, M. C. (ed.) (1977). *O Frabjous Day! Poetry for Holidays and Special Occasions*. New York: Atheneum. ISBN 0 689 50076 9   Divided into three thematic units which 'celebrate', 'honor' and 'remember', this anthology contains poetry from the first century to the present, by poets from America, China, Japan, England, Ireland, Scotland, Israel, Rome and Germany.

Native North-American Poetry

An excellent guide to contemporary native American poetry is: Wiget, A. (1984). 'Sending a voice: the emergence of contemporary native American poetry', *College English*, **46** (6) October. Two important anthologies are:

Rosen, K. (ed.) (1975). *Voices of the Rainbow*. New York: Viking.
Duane Niatum, D. (ed.) (1981). *Carriers of the Dream Wheel*. New York: Harper and Row.

Audio-visual resources

There are several films, videos, records and audio-tapes of poets' readings, readings by actors, autobiographical and biographical pieces, and productions centred around specific poems. The following list is a small sample of such items.

Film and video

Autumn: Frost Country. Pyramid Film and Video, Box 1048, Santa Monica, CA 90406   Write to Pyramid for further details on other films/videos, including 'Once by the Pacific' (Frost) and 'A Certain Slant of Light' (Dickinson).

e. e. cummings: The Making of a Poet. Films for the Humanities, Box 2053, Princeton, N.J. 08540   Self-portrait in the poet's own voice, poetry, painting and notebooks (24 min., video (VHS and Beta) and 16 mm film).

Emily Dickinson: A Certain Slant of Light. International Film Bureau.   Julie Harris narrates and reads (29 min., film).

Robert Frost: A First Acquaintance. Films for the Humanities, Box 2053, Princeton, N.J. 08540   Frost reads and talks about poetry with students – some of his best known poems (16 min., video (VHS and Beta) and 16 mm film).

Donald Hall at Eagle Pond Farm. Paradigm Video, Inc., 6205 Guilford, Canton, Michigan 48187   Hall recites his poetry and talks about 'connections' at the Farm (30 min., video – VHS).

Ezra Pound, Poet's Poet. Films for the Humanities, Box 2053, Princeton, N.J. 08540   Pound in this 80s retraces his life and reads some of his poems (29 min., video (VHS and Beta) and 16 mm film).

Wallace Stevens and *The Sound of Poetry: Green and Blue* (Wallace Stevens)   Both films are distributed by Doubleday.

Audiotapes and records

Two major distributors of recorded readings are Caedmon and Spoken Arts. Worth noting are *Poetry of Langston Hughes* (Caedmon TC 1272) and *e. e. cummings Reads His Poetry* (Caedmon TC 1017). Readings by Roethke are available on *Words for the Wind* (Folkways 9736). Write to Caedmon, 1995 Broadway, New York, N.Y. 10023.

Watershed Tapes (P.O. Box 50145, Washington, D.C. 20004) has a large listing of contemporary poets reading their own poetry. Among them are William Dickey, Lawrence Ferlinghetti, Stanley Kunitz, Denise Levertov, Kenneth Rexroth, Muriel Rukeyeser, William Stafford and Reed Whittemore.

People resources

Most States run Poets in the Schools Programs through such organizations as the Councils for the Arts and Humanities.

Bibliography

Andrew, R. (1983). *Into Poetry*. London: Ward Lock Education.

Applebee, A. N. (1977). The elements of response to a literary work: what we have learned. *Research in the Teaching of English*, **11**, 255–71.

Barnes, D. (1976). *From Communication to Curriculum*. Harmondsworth, Middlesex: Penguin Books.

Barnes, D., Churley, P. and Thompson, C. (1971). Group talk and literary response. *English in Education*, **5** (3), 63–76.

Barthes, R. (1974). *S/Z* (translated by R. Miller). New York: Hill and Wang.

Bartlett, F. C. (1932). *Remembering*. Cambridge: Cambridge University Press.

Beach, R. W. (1972). The Literary Response Process of College Students while Reading and Discussing Three Poems. Ph.D. dissertation, University of Illinois at Urbana. *D.A.I.*, **34**.

Blackie, P. (1971). Asking questions. *English in Education*, **5** (3), 77–9.

Bleich, D. (1975). *Readings and Feelings: An Introduction to Subjective Criticism*. Urbana, Ill.: NCTE.

Bleich, D. (1978). *Subjective Criticism*. Baltimore: John Hopkins University Press.

Britton, J. N. (1954). Evidence of improvement in poetic judgement. *British Journal of Educational Psychology*, **45**, 196–208.

Britton, J. N. (1972). *Language and Learning*. Harmondsworth, Middlesex: Penguin Books.

Brownjohn, S. (1980). *Does It Have to Rhyme?* London: Hodder and Stoughton.

Bruner, J. S. (1966). *Toward a Theory of Instruction*. Cambridge, Mass.: Harvard University Press.

Bryant, C. (1984). Teaching students to read poetry independently: An experiment in bringing together research and the teacher. *English Quarterly*, **17** (4), 48–57.

Ciardi, J. (1959). *How Does a Poem Mean?* Boston: Houghton Mifflin Co.

Commission on English (1965). *Freedom and Discipline in English*. New York: College Entrance Examination Board.

Craig, G. (1976). Reading: who is doing what to whom? *In* Josipovici, G. (ed.), *The Modern English Novel: The Reader, the Writer, and the Work*, pp. 15–36. London: Open Books Publishing Ltd.

Culler, J. (1975). *Structuralist Poetics: Structuralism, Linguistics and the Study of Literature*. London: Routledge and Kegan Paul.

Culler, J. (1981). *The Pursuit of Signs: Semiotics, Literature, Deconstruction*. London: Routledge and Kegan Paul.

Culler, J. (1983). *On Deconstruction: Theory and Criticism after Structuralism*. London: Routledge and Kegan Paul.

de Beaugrande, R. (1984). Writer, reader, critic: Comparing critical theories as discourse. *College English*, **46** (6), 533–59.

Department of Education and Science (1975). *A Language for Life*. London: HMSO.

Department of Education and Science (1987). *Teaching Poetry in the Secondary School: An HMI View*. London: HMSO.

Dias, P. (1979). Developing independent readers of poetry: An approach in the high school. *McGill Journal of Education*, **14**, 199–214.

Dias, P. (1987). *Making Sense of Poetry: Patterns in the Process*. Ottawa: Canadian Council of Teachers of English.

van Dijk, T. and Kintsch, W. (1983). *Strategies of Discourse Comprehension*. London: Academic Press.

Dillon, G. (1978). *Language Processing and the Reading of Literature: Toward a Model of Comprehension*. Bloomington, Indiana: Indiana University Press.

Dillon, G. (1980). Discourse processing and the nature of literary narrative. *Poetics*, **9**, 163–80.

Dixon, J. (1967). *Growth through English*. Oxford: Oxford University Press.

Dixon, J. (1974). Formulation in group discussion. *Educational Review* (Birmingham), **26**, 241–50.

Dixon, J. and Brown, J. (1985). *Responses to Literature: What Is Being Assessed?*, Parts 1 and 2. London: SCDC Publications.

Eagleton, T. (1983). *Literary Theory: An Introduction*. Oxford: Blackwell.

Eco, U. (1979). *The Role of the Reader: Explorations in the Semiotics of Text*. Bloomington, Indiana: Indiana University Press.

Fish, S. (1980). *Is There a Text in This Class?* Cambridge, Mass.: Harvard University Press.

Frye, N. 1966. *Anatomy of Criticism*. New York: Atheneum.

Goodman, K. (1967). Reading: A psycholinguistic guessing game. *Journal of the Reading Specialist*, **6**, 126–35.

Graves, D. H. (1981). Renters and owners: Donald Graves on writing. *The English Magazine*, **8**, 4–7.

Greeves, A. (1986). What, no daffodils? *The Times Educational Supplement*, (London), 19 September, p. 22.

Grugeon, E. and Walden, P. (eds) (1978). *Literature and Learning*. London: Ward Lock Educational.

Halliday, M. A. K. and Hasan, R. (1976). *Cohesion in English*. London: Longman.

Harding, D. W. (1937). The role of the onlooker. *Scrutiny*, **6**, 247–58.

Harding, D. W. (1968). Practice at liking: A study in experimental aesthetics. *Bulletin of the British Psychological Society*, **21** (70), 3–10.

Harris, R. and McFarlane, P. (1983). *A Book to Write Poems By*. Adelaide: Australian Association for the Teaching of English.

Harris, R. and McFarlane, P. (1985). *A Book to Perform Poems By*. Adelaide: Australian Association for the Teaching of English.

Holland, N. (1973). *Poems in Persons: An Introduction to the Psychoanalysis of Literature*. New York: W. W. Norton.

Holland, N. (1975). *5 Readers Reading*. New Haven: Yale University Press.

Holland, N. (1985). Reading readers reading. *In* Cooper, C. (ed.), *Researching Response to Literature and the Teaching of Literature: Points of Departure*, pp. 3–21. Norwood, N.J.: Ablex Publishing.

Hughes, T. (1969). *Poetry in the Making*. London: Faber and Faber.

Ingham, J. (1981). *Books and Reading Development*. London: Heinemann Educational.

Iser, W. (1978). *The Act of Reading: A Theory of Aesthetic Response*. Baltimore: John Hopkins University Press.

Jackson, D. (1982). *Continuity in Secondary English*. London: Methuen.

Josipovici, G. (1977). *The Lessons of Modernism*. London: Macmillan.

Knights, L. C. (1964). In search of fundamental values. In *The Critical Moment: Literary Criticism in the 1960s*. Essays from the *London Times Literary Supplement*. New York: McGraw-Hill.

Koch, K. (1973). *Rose, Where Did You Get That Red?* New York: Vintage Books.

Langer, S. K. (1953). *Feeling and Form*. New York: Charles Scribner's Sons.

Lanham, R. A. (1983). One, two, three. *In* Horner, W. B. (ed.), *Composition and Literature: Bridging the Gap*. Chicago: The University of Chicago Press.

Leavis, F. R. (1948). *Education and the University*. London: Chatto and Windus.

Leavis, F. R. (1962). *Two Cultures? The Significance of C. P. Snow*. London: Chatto and Windus.

Martin, N. *et al.* (1976). *Writing and Learning across the Curriculum*. London: Ward Lock Educational.

Meek, M. (1983). *Achieving Literacy: Longitudinal Studies of Adolescents Learning to Read*. London: Routledge and Kegan Paul.

Mills, R. W. (1974). Small group discussion. *English in Education*, **8**, 10–21.

Milton, J. (1644). *Aeropagitica*.

Minsky, M. (1975). A framework for representing knowledge. *In* Winston, P. H. (ed.), *The Psychology of Computer Vision*. New York: McGraw-Hill.

Ong, W. (1975). The writer's audience is always a fiction. *PMLA*, **90**, 9–21.

Propp, V. (1970). *Morphology of the Folktale*. Austin, Texas: University of Texas Press (first published in 1928).

Purves, A. (1973). *Literature Education in Ten Countries*. Stockholm: Almquist and Wiksell.

Purves, A. and Rippere, V. (1968). *Elements of Writing about a Literary Work: A Study of Response to Literature*. Urbana, Ill.: NCTE.

Reid, I. (1984). *The Making of Literature*. Adelaide: Australian Association for the Teaching of English.

Richards, I. A. (1929). *Practical Criticism*. New York: Harcourt, Brace and World, Inc.

Riffaterre, M. (1978). *Semiotics of Poetry*. Bloomington, Indiana: Indiana University Press.

Rosenblatt, L. (1938). *Literature as Exploration*. New York: Appleton-Century.

Rosenblatt, L. (1978). *The Reader, the Text, the Poem*. Carbondale, Ill.: Southern Illinois University Press.

Schank, R. C. and Abelson, R. (1977). *Scripts, Plans, Goals, and Understanding*. Hillsdale, N.J.: Lawrence Erlbaum.

Slatoff, W. (1970). *With Respect to Readers: Dimensions of Literary Response*. Ithaca: Cornell University Press.

Smith, F. (1978). *Understanding Reading*, 2nd ed. New York: Holt, Rinehart and Winston.

Smith, F. (1985). A metaphor for literacy: creating worlds or shunting information. *In* Olson, D. R., Torrance, N. and Hildyard, A. (eds), *Literacy, Language, and Learning: The Nature and Consequences of Reading and Writing*. Cambridge: Cambridge University Press.

Spiro, R. J. (1982). Long-term comprehension: Schema-based versus experiential and evaluative understanding. *Poetics*, 11, 77–86.

Squire, J. R. (ed) (1968). Response to literature. Champaign, Ill.; NCTE.

Stratta, L., Dixon, J. and Wilkinson, A. (1973). *Patterns of Language: Explorations in the Teaching of English*. London: Heinemann Educational.

Tillyard, E. M. W. (1945). *Poetry, Direct and Oblique* (revised edition). London: Chatto and Windus.

Todorov, T. (1980). Reading as construction. *In* Suleiman, S. R. and Crosman, I. (eds), *The Reader in the Text*, pp. 67–82. Princeton, N.J.: Princeton University Press.

Torbe, M. (1974). Modes of response: Some interactions between reader and literature. *English in Education*, 8, 21–32.

Travers, D. M. M. (1982). Problems in writing about poetry and some solutions. *English in Education*, 16 (3), 55–65.

Webb, K. (1979). *I Like This Poem*. Harmondsworth, Middlesex: Penguin.

Widdowson, H. G. (1975). *Stylistics and the Teaching of Literature*. London: Longman.

Wimsatt, W. K., Jr (1958). *The Verbal Icon: Studies in the Meaning of Poetry*. New York: Noonday Press.

Index